J. C Trott

A Collection of Poems and Songs

Descriptive, Sentimental & Humorous

J. C Trott

A Collection of Poems and Songs
Descriptive, Sentimental & Humorous

ISBN/EAN: 9783337006723

Printed in Europe, USA, Canada, Australia, Japan

Cover: Foto ©Thomas Meinert / pixelio.de

More available books at **www.hansebooks.com**

A COLLECTION OF

POEMS AND SONGS

DESCRIPTIVE, SENTIMENTAL & HUMOROUS

BY

J. C. TROTT.

HALIFAX:
"GUARDIAN" PRINTING WORKS, GEORGE STREET.

1895.

CONTENTS.

	Page.		Page.
To Poetry	1	The Young	65
To a Violet	2	The Portrait of a Critic	67
To a Daisy	3	A Quiet Mind	69
Thou Art Passing Away	4	Consider the Flowers	70
Love	5	Trip to the Isle of Man	71
The Masher O	6	The Parting	73
To a Buttercup	7	An Aged Pilgrim	74
'Tis Better on Before	8	Waifs and Strays	75
A Tribute	10	Morn	76
Norah Doone	12	Experience	77
An Old Old Story	12	To a Rose	78
Carpe Diem	15	Faded Leaves	79
The People's Park	16	The Spirit of Spring	80
At Home	19	The Return to Wisdom	81
Nature's School	20	The Hero	86
The Snow	21	The Green Dell	88
Speak the Truth	22	"Guardian" v. "Courier"	89
The Power of Kindness	23	Night Thoughts	90
The Solo Boy	24	A Tribute	93
A Literary Tragedy	26	The Poet's World	94
A November Day	27	A Pastoral	95
The Mermaids	28	Poverty	96
Robert Burns	29	A Jingle	98
A True Man	31	Where are the Nine?	99
The Forest	32	An Autumn Memory	100
The Reprieve	33	The Gift of Poetry	102
My Little Boy Who Died	34	The Priest's Secret	103
Guardian Angels	36	A Voice from the Sky	106
A Birthday Wish	36	A Life Thought	108
General Gordon	37	The First Psalm	109
A Political Ballad	38	The New Year	109
Pleasures	39	Burlesque v. The Drama	111
Tho' Far From Thee	39	A Word of Consolation	114
The First Kiss	40	The Winter Months of '95	116
May and December	40	Life	117
Autumn	41	To Scotland	118
Practical Sympathy	42	The Poet's Joy	119
True Nobility	43	A Night Reverie	120
'Tis the Voice of the Comp.	44	A Greeting	122
Descent is Easy	45	A Song	123
The Special Correspondent	46	Deeds versus Creeds	124
O Never Say Die!	48	The Day is Dark and Dreary	125
Evening	49	A Midnight Cat-astrophe	126
The Lay of the Lost Minstrel	51	"Faithful unto Death"	128
Spring	52	A Christmas Story	129
Bradford v. Halifax	54	Verbum Sap.	134
Life's Alchemy	55	A Prologue	134
Only a Circus Clown	56	The Constant Heart	136
An Invocation to Nature	58	Be Still	136
Who is My Neighbour?	60	The Bee	137
Speak no Ill	61	A Ballad	137
Actin' Webb	62	The Flight of Summer	138
Charity	63	A Tribute	139

CONTENTS.

	Page.		Page.
For Love and Chivalry	140	The True Politician	170
The Jester's Love	141	To Peace	171
Till Death do part	142	O Sing those Songs Again	172
A Lament	143	Daffodils	173
Carissimma	143	In the Gloaming	174
The Tale of Life	144	The Girl I Loved Long Years	
My True Love	146	Ago	175
The Lady of the Land	147	Rules of Life	175
The Jester	148	Christmas is Here	176
The Tale of Love	150	The Sea	178
Drive Them Back over the Water	151	The Buccaneer	178
Tarry Not	152	The Wind	180
Memory	152	The Little Messenger	182
He Has Gone	154	Earth and Heaven	184
Life's Inequalities	155	Hope	185
The Emigrant Ship	156	A Life Thought	187
My Lady Sleeps	158	A Greeting	189
Sleep, Calmly Sleep	159	"Ave Maria"	189
The Lovers	160	The World's Needs	190
The Idiot Lad	164	England's Duke is Satisfied	192
Our Gifts	166	Only an Old Old Ditty	192
The Old Year	161	The Hours of Life	193
My Love	167	Sonnets	194
Fancyland	168	To a Disappointed Genius	195
The Author's Aspiration	169		

LIST OF SUBSCRIBERS.

Abraham, H. J., Parish Church Choir	1
Ashworth, Normanton, Gibbet Street	1
Almond, W., 1, Milton Terrace	1
Almond, C., do.	1
Ackroyd, W., Borough Analyst	2
Angus, Mrs. G., 9, Pembroke Street, Glasgow	1
Atter, J. A., 5, Knight Street	1
Ashworth, Mrs. F., 39, Holly Grove	1
Ansteed, W., Theatre Royal	1
Brooke, The Ven. Archdeacon, The Vicarage	5
Blatchford, M. J.,	5
Barber, L. C., "Guardian" Office	1
Bates, M., do.	1
Beaver, W. H., do.	1
Berry, J. (Messrs. Helliwell's, Crown Street)	1
Balmforth, William Ernest, "Guardian" Office	1
Barnes, A., Parish Church Choir	1
Bentley, Robinson, Dean Clough	1
Bedford, Charles, Mount Street	1
Brearley, T. H., Parish Church Choir	1
Burke, G., do.	1
Bentley, H., do.	1
Brookes, W., do.	1
Binns, J. V., do.	1
Blakey, Alfred, do.	1
Beverley, B., do.	1
Bailey, Ernest, 7, Manor Drive	1
Bates, James (Messrs. Walton's, Square)	1
Brier, J., Woolshops	1
Bentley, J. Tasker, 10, Victor Terrace	1
Bowman, H. H., J.P., Savile Grove	1
Brook, J., Post Office	1
Bowles, J. J. (My Bootmakers)	1
Bowker, C., Kingston	1
Bairstow, J. (Messrs. Seed Brothers)	1
Bromwich, Miss, Raglan Street	1
Beton, Hy. E., Heathfield Place	1
Birtwhistle, W. H., Lower Cross Street	1
Bell, Henry, Cash Supply Stores	1
Brook, William, Waterhouse Street	1
Bailey, W., Solicitor, Waterhouse Street	1
Bulmer, T. Edgar, Willow Bank	1
Bottomley, Robert, 17, Milton Terrace	1
Clucas, Charles, Grand Theatre	1
Crabtree, Edward, "Guardian" Office	1
Couldwell, J. W., Wards End	1
Crabtree, W., Conservative Union	3
Collins, J., Parish Church Choir	1
Crossland, J. H.	1

LIST OF SUBSCRIBERS.

Cooke, William, Bull Green
Coates, Lister, George Street
Crowther, T. G., Parish Church Choir
Cooper, J. H.,   do.
Cliff, J., Barum Top
Cockroft, Ernest, Post Office
Clayton, J. S., Kingston
Crossley, J. E., Craven Terrace
Crawshaw, J. H., Earl Street
Cotton, A., Yorkshire Penny Bank
Copley, Wright, Rose Street,
Collinson, T., J.P., Waterhouse Street
Collinson, E., St. John's Place
Collins, Mrs., 17, Dumbarton Road, Glasgow
Cawthra, J. S., 3, Gladstone Road

Douglas-Hamilton, Rev. H. A., Holy Trinity Vicarage
Dunstan, W. H., Parish Church Choir
Dennis, J. R., Dean Clough
Dobson, — (Messrs. Simpson & Son)
Dixon, H., Argyle Press
Dobson, C., Craven Edge
Denham, W., St. James' Street
Davenport, Thomas, 46, St. Augustine's Terrace
Dolan, Dr. T. M., Horton House
Drake, H., Akroydon
Dobson, G. G., 8, Lewis Street

Earnshaw, S., Ferguson Street

Fielding, L., "Guardian" Office
Fleming, F., The Boulevards
Fleming, J. A., Pellon Place
Fleming, J. W., Corn Market
Fish, W. H.
Foster, H. E., Solicitor, George Street
Foster, J. W., Square Chapel
Fox, C. J., Architect, George Street
Foster, Frank, "Guardian" Office
Foster, J. W.,   do.
Farr, J., Crown Street

Greenwood, F., "Guardian" Office
Garland, W. H., The Boulevards
Gibbs, W. P., Post Office
Garside, J. E., (Mr. Walshaw's, Northgate)
Gaukroger, W., J.P., Fernside
Gordon, Canon, St. Marie's Rectory
Graydon, Rawdon, 30, Southgate
Garside, G. E., King Cross Street
Greenwood, J. W., Parish Church Choir

Haigh, W., 31, Stirling Street
Halcrow, J., "Guardian" Office

LIST OF SUBSCRIBERS.

Heap, W., (Mr. Learoyd's)
Horsley, F., Cross Hills Coal Club
Halliday, J. E., Northgate (Mr. Fawthrop's)
Huntriss, E., Hopwood Hall
Hitchen, J. H., Parish Church Choir
Hey, C. H., Bull Green
Higgins, C. A., Bull Green
Hadfield, J. R., Technical School
Hall, Dr. J. W., Moor Royd
Halliday, John, St. Augustine's Schools
Holroyd, B., Parish Church Choir
Higden, W. H., Holy Trinity School
Hatch, J. J., Central Hall
Hanson, Ehud, Clare Road
Horsfall, Richard, Stoodley House
Hogg, John, Brunswick Street
Hey, Hanson, Battinson Road
Haigh, Miss, 2, West Grove, Wellington Street
Halliwell, J. D., 3, Pear Street, Kingston
Halliday, J., 67, Clare Road
Harper, B., Pellon Lane
Hallas, Gledhill, Stainland
Holdsworth, W., Auctioneer, Northgate
Haigh, W. (Messrs. Carver & Co.)
Hill, E. H., Harrison Road
Henderson, Rev. R. A., Parish Church
Holt, James, 34, Hyde Park Road
Hirst, David, Baines Street
Hird, Rev. H. G., St. Mary's Vicarage

Ibberson, C. W., John Street
Illingworth, T., Crown Street
Imbery, J., 16, Hyde Park Road

Jackson, W., Post Office
Jowett, J. E., Osborn Terrace, Queen's Road
Jackson, J. W., Sanitary Department
Johnstone, Rev. A., Park Place

King, J. W., "Guardian" Office
Kitchen, T.,   do.
Knowles, J., Gibbet Street
Kerr, J. R., Square
Kershaw, Leonard, County Court
Knights, Miss H., 25, Savile Crescent
Kershaw, J. B., Fountain Street
Kirk, Major, Harrison Road

Lister, H., Hanson Lane
Lewthwaite, Rev. T., All Souls' Vicarage
Lawrence, John, Green Lane
Lister, J., M.A., C.C., Shibden Hall
Learoyd, J. I., Commercial Street

IV. LIST OF SUBSCRIBERS.

Lawrence, Frank, Green Lane
Lent, Walter, King Cross
Littlefield, A., 2, Bedford Street, Gibbet Street
Lowe, E., Russell Street
Linley, J., West Hill Park
Lister, A., 31, New Road

Mumby, C., " Guardian " Office
Manson, W. Innes, Lightcliffe..
Marchant, J. C., Dean Clough
Morton, J., Pellon Lane
Mitchell, David, Griffin Hotel..
Morton, S., Parish Church Choir
Mitchell, F., Wards End
Mitchell, J., Dean Clough
Mitchell, Louis, 37, Swinton Terrace
Maude, Richard, Aked's Road..
Mitchell, W. H., Wards End
Mitchell, J., Kingston
Millson, Rev. F. E., Balmoral Place
Mackrell, J., Hopwood Lane
Marsh, G., Silver Street
Milligan, George, Organist
McNicoll, Dr., Manchester Road, Southport
Martin, W., Falcon Laundry
Midgley, W., Harrison Road
Mahony, E., North Parade
Moore, H. E., Holmfield
Mitchell, J. H., Greetland

Naylor, G., Post Office
Normanton, J. W., St. James' Road
North, George, Crown Street
Nettleton, A., Dean Clough
Neville, J. L., Theatre Royal
Normington, J., 37, Violet Street

Oates, W. H., Stirling Street
Oates, George Alfred, Bangor Street
Oliver, A., 33, Milton Street
Ogden, J. H., " Guardian " Office
Ogden, A. E.,   do.
Osler, Rev. C. H., Parish Church

Priestley, T., North Bridge
Priestley, J., Waterhouse Street
Pritchard, Charles, Portland Place
Patterson, W. A., Milton Place
Pickles, Miss, Messrs. Seed Bros.
Patchett, J. J., Alma Street
Pole, C., Town Hall
Parkyn, Rev. N. L., Lightcliffe

LIST OF SUBSCRIBERS. V.

Ratcliffe, J. W., "Guardian" Office 1
Reeves, H., do. 1
Robinson, W., Roebuck Yard 1
Ratcliffe, Albert, Horley Green Road, Claremount 1
Rowe Miss, Gladstone Road 1
Rowe, Rev. G. F. H., Gladstone Road 1
Roper, Frank, North Parade 1
Robertshaw, Misses, Parliament Street 1
Robinson, —, Parish Church Choir 1
Renton, Miss, 25, Savile Crescent 1
Rhodes, C., Silver Street 1
Riley, J. T., J.P., Savile Lea 1
Robertshaw, J., Town Hall 1
Riley, T., Post Office 1
Rouse, C. H., Norfolk Place 1
Rigden, E., 55, Caledonia Road, Glasgow.. 1
Robinson, Henry, Bank House 1
Reid, T. M., Crown Street 1
Rawnsley, G. R., Waterhouse Street 1
Riley, G. M., Commercial Street 1
Roberts, John, Bell Hall 1
Robertshaw, Mrs., Back Gerrard Street 1

Sutcliffe, J., "Guardian" Office 1
Sandie, R. W., "Guardian" Office 1
Shaw, E., Post Office 1
Seed, Joseph, Crown Street 1
Seed, Tom do. 1
Seed, Alfred do. 1
Seed, George do. 1
Seed, Albert do. 2
Smith, David, Haley Hill 1
Simpson, C., Akroydon 1
Seed, Walter 1
Sladdin, J., Gladstone Road 2
Sykes, — 1
Storey, Walter, King Cross Street 2
Spencer, Councillor W. H. 3
Spencer, Councillor J. T. 5
Shepley, Harry 1
Smith, Thos., Holly Grove 1
Smith, Rev. M. C., Parish Church 2
Scarf, J. Holly Grove 1
Sheard, —, Messrs. Bracken & Co. 1
Sharpe, G. F., Crossley Street.. 1
Smith, Adam, Heath View 1
Singleton, R. H., Chester Road 1
Smith, Mrs. M. A., 10, Prince Edward Street, Glasgow .. 1
Smith, Thomas do. do. .. 1
Smith, Miss R. B. do. do. .. 1
Smith, Miss Lily do. do. .. 1

LIST OF SUBSCRIBERS.

Shaw, S. V., Commercial Street	1
Swale, J. S., 19. King Cross Street	1
Stott, J. W., Post Office	1
Stubbs, T., do.	1
Sladdin, J., 3, Holden Street	1
Stafford, R. P., King Cross Street	1
Stock, Rev. W. L., 16, Trooper Lane	1
Smith, Councillor G. H., The Gleddings	1
Smith, W. J., School House, Thelfall	1
Spencer, W. B., Governor Street	1
Taylor, C., Parish Church Choir,	1
Tetlaw, Handel, 25, Hanover Street	1
Topham, Dr. A. S., Fountain Street	5
Taylor, E. T., Post Office	1
Thornton, A. G., Broad Road, Sale, Cheshire	1
Taylor, J. D., Princess Street	1
Trott, R., 15, Edward Street, Deptford	1
Utley, Samuel, C.E., Norfolk Place	1
Walker, Mrs. T. J., 25, Savile Crescent	2
White, J. H., " Guardian " Office	1
Wilson, A., do.	1
Whiteley, G., do.	1
Wade, S. T., Roseberry Terrace	1
Wilson, T., Gibbet Street	1
Whitaker, Ald. J., Craven Lodge	1
West-Symes, Dr. E., Hope Hall	1
Walsh, C., Co-operative Stores	2
Wormald Miss	1
Whitehead, J., Moorland Terrace	1
Wilson, E., George Street	1
Winter, Rev. E., Elland	1
Womersley, W. C., Wade Street	1
Wild, T., Stannary	1
Walshaw, J., Northgate	1
Winter, J. W., The Boulevards	1
Williamson, J., Station Bookstall	1
Waddington, J. H., Draper	1
Whiteley, W., St. James' Road	1
White, Councillor W.	1
Workman, F., Gibbet Street	1
Williams, W. C., George Street	1
Wood, J. S., "Courier" Office	1
Wilkinson, Robert, Fountain Street	1
Walton Keighley, The Woodlands	2
Webster, C. E., Silver Street	1
Wainhouse, William, King Cross Street	1
Wright, Dr. J. Crossley, Park Road	1
Worsnop, A., Wards End	1

PREFACE.

In submitting this collection of Poems and Songs to public consideration, I desire first of all to thank the numerous subscribers whose generous support has rendered possible the achievement of a long-cherished desire.

With regard to the work itself, I trust it will be found that in the various subjects treated of I have not attempted flights beyond my powers, but that, remembering the old saying that "fools rush in where angels fear to tread," I have pursued the *via media* of safety, and confined myself to efforts well within the scope of my capabilities. Although probably the severely classical may be unable to discern much to either gratify the taste or appeal to the intellect, still I venture to hope the general run of readers will be able to derive both pleasure and profit, and also feel in the different portrayals of human character and experience that "touch of nature that makes the whole world kin."

Painfully conscious of my many deficiencies, I must ask the reader's kind indulgence for any errors in construction or other little literary blemishes that may present themselves.

Trusting that my humble efforts may commend themselves to your favourable consideration,

I remain,

Yours respectfully,

J. C. TROTT.

TO POETRY.

SWEET Poesy, if thy bright light
    But beam upon my way,
This soul of mine can know no night;
    But, bless'd by thine Aeonian ray,
Unbroken, cloudless, endless day.

If but thy precious priceless gift
    My lowly soul possess,
I have a lever that can lift
    My heart above the ills that press
In this drear mundane wilderness.

Let but thy thrilling tuneful lay
    Fall on my ravish'd ear,
All worldly tumults die away;
    Then swiftly discord, doubt, and fear
Vanish to more congenial sphere.

With thine inspiring matchless fire
    O touch each "trembling string"
Of my poor uninstructed lyre,
    And various tuneful strains forth bring,
Music's sweet soul awakening.

Kind Muse, my Alma Mater be,
    'Neath thy benignant rule,
Taught in thy great academy,
    Wise shall I grow tho' deemed a fool
By this world's cold prosaic school.

Could I but wield thy facile brush,
    What pictures wondrous rare
Would I portray—the crimson blush
    Of placid evening mildly fair—
Or morning grand beyond compare!

Then beauteous Spirit, O dispense
    Thy wonder-working power;
The fervour rich, the bliss intense
    Of thy unpurchaseable dower—
Poesy's amaranthine flower.

TO A VIOLET.

CHILD of obscurity,
   Nestling in purity
  In the green dell;
Hid in thy lone retreat,
Scatt'ring thy perfume sweet
  Where flowerets dwell.

Mantl'd in modest grace,
In thee my thought can trace
  Type of that mind
Which far from mortal ken,
Far from the haunts of men,
  Noble and kind,

Spends all Life's fleeting hours,
All of its varying powers,
  In noble ways;
Shedding a fragrance round
Earth's saddest, darkest ground,
  Seeking no praise.

Unknown, unrecognis'd,
Often but little priz'd,
  Lowly, obscure;
Cradl'd in low estate,
Scorn'd by the rich, the great,
  Worthy tho' poor.

Bloom on, dear lowly flower,
So may the Heavenly Power
  Teach us, that we
May thy sweet worth discern,
And the grand lesson learn
  Taught us by thee.

TO A DAISY.

SWEET flow'ret, clad in snowy white,
  Or in a vest of crimson bright,
Meekly raising thy pure head
From thy scented, verdant bed;
Gazing up with reverent eye
To the vast expanse of sky—
In simple trusting innocence
Appealing to Omnipotence
To grant thy tiny life a share
In His all-embracing care.
Happy in thy lowly state,
Careless thou of Time or Fate;
The poet's pet, a brilliant gem
In fair Flora's diadem.
Teacher great in humble guise—
Teaching alike foolish, wise;
Preacher thou most eloquent—
Preaching lowliness; content,
Thankful when the sun's bright smile
Woos thy blushing face awhile;
Uncomplainingly resign'd,
When the angry tyrant wind
Rudely smites thy trembling cheek
Ever trustful, hopeful, meek,
In thee a lesson deep we see
Of patience in adversity—
Hoping on for brighter days,
Cheery skies and sunshine's rays.
O lowly daisy, e'er in thee,
A bright example may we see;
Like thee may we be meek and pure,
Be patient hardship to endure,
Resigned unto His sovereign will,
Whose power the universe doth fill.

THOU ART PASSING AWAY.

THOU art passing away, but we will not deplore thee,
    Though sorely it grieveth us from thee to part,
When we think of the glory that lies on before thee,
    With humble submission we see thee depart.

Thou art passing away, and we would not recall thee
    To this land of sorrow e'en had we the power;
On that tranquil shore no ills can befall thee;
    No trouble-charg'd clouds upon thee e'er lour

Thou art passing away, hands rev'rent and tender
    Shall clothe thy still form for its last narrow bed,
And a grief-stricken train shall solemnly render
    The last that affection can do for the dead.

Thou art passing away, through the glittering portals,
    To the bright golden streets and the gem-sparkling plain,
Where the rapturous hosts of redeemed immortals
    Make the balmy air ring with their ceaseless refrain.

Thou art passing away, but we in our sorrow,
    Should not mourn over thee as those without hope,
But patiently wait the Eternal to-morrow,
    Heav'n aiding us well with our trial to cope.

Thou art passing away, and we too must follow
    And quit this vain region of transient delight;
Earth's goodliest things, how poor and how hollow
    Appear they when view'd in Eternity's light!

Thou art passing away, and, blessed assurance—
    Through our Father's great love we may meet thee again:
How the hope fills our bosom with strength and endurance,
    And aids us to carry our burden of pain!

LOVE.

WHAT force in the world is so potent as love !
    The tempest may fright us, the earthquake remove,
The roll of the thunder our minds may appal ;
But love is a power greater stronger than all.

Scare a being on earth but his sovereignty owns ;
He sways like a despot proud kings on their thrones ;
He rules the poor peasant who sighs in the grove,
As his heart vainly strives with the power of love.

O Cupid ! a ruthless young tyrant thou art,
Inflicting deep wounds with thy random-sent dart ;
How often thou banishest sleep from the eyes,
As vainly to woo it some poor lover tries ;
Go seek where ye will, ye never shall find
A monarch who wieldeth more sway o'er Mankind.

Go ask if you will yon proud millionaire—
Why he roams through his grounds with so pensive an air ;
Why so troubl'd his mien, so haggard his face ?
Why he wanders alone at so laggard a pace ?
And the pet child of Fortune's sad answer shall prove
The exquisite tortures inflicted by Love.

Ask too that brave sailor boy high on the mast,
As the stout vessel trembles and reels in the blast,
What is it that keeps him so calm 'mid the storm ?
And he'll own with a blush—the sweet features and form
Of a dearly loved maid, like an angel of light,
Shine clear on his path through the tempest's dark night ;
And as the good ship through the boiling surf moves,
He is cheer'd by the thought of the sweetheart he loves.

And have we not seen, too, the bold son of Mars
Return home unscathed from the peril of wars
To be vanquish'd at once by Beauty's bright glance,
And yield at first prick of the young tyrant's lance !
How that bosom as firm as his cuirass of steel,
That never a tremor of terror did feel
When bullet and sabre assail'd him in vain
Hath been wounded and torn by Love's blissful pain !

Ask that child of sweet fancies as by the lone stream
He thoughtfully roves—what's his favourite theme?
And his face will be wreath'd with a halo of light,
As he smilingly answers, Love's heavenly delight;
Yes he sings "la grandè passion" so wondrously strong,
Yes love is the bard's sweetest, favourite song.

THE MASHER O.
(After Burns—A considerable distance.)

HEIGHO the Masher O
    The tight-panted Masher O
If there is ought amazes me
It is the modern Masher O.

The curly-brimmed hat Masher O
The street-parading Masher O
Bowing to "Totties" whom he meets,
The lady-killing Masher O.

The fashion-watching Masher O
The "jam-pot" collar'd Masher O
With "eyeglass in his ocular,"
The empty-headed Masher O.

The leering, ogling Masher O
The bar-frequenting Masher O
Spending his father's hard won-pelf,
The trade-despising Masher O.

The idle, worthless Masher O
The *blasè*, rakish Masher O
'Twas Nature who produced the man,
But "brass" produc'd the Masher O.

The art-affecting Masher O
The Wilde-adoring Masher O
The quite too utterly intense,
The "high" æsthetic Masher O.

Heigho the Masher O
O would to God the Masher O
Might be a useful manly man,
And cease to be a Masher O!

TO A BUTTERCUP.

DEAR flow'ret, sorrow fills my breast,
    As I survey thy golden crest,
That erst on Nature's velvet vest
          So brightly shone,
By Ruin's ruthless power oppress'd,
          Thy beauty gone.

Bright darling of the rural glade,
In sweet simplicity arrayed,
O'er thee fond zephyrs as they stray'd
          Made music sweet,
Alas! now mangled 'neath the tread
          Of passing feet.

We saw thee e'er reviving Spring
Came forth on rainbow-tinted wing
To metamorphose everything,
          A courier gay—
Nature's pursuivant, heralding
          Approaching May.

When merry-hearted buxom May
Beam'd brightly on the prospect gray,
And thickly drap'd hedgerow and spray
          In blossom white,
She smil'd on thee, her fav'rite fay,
          With deep delight.

When Summer ope'd his golden reign,
Clothing in radiant tints the plain,
And Flora, with a beauteous chain
          Deck'd field and bower.
We saw thee foremost in her train,
          Thou pretty flower.

As summer clouds that melt away
Before the sun's all powerful ray,
So transient was thy life's brief day—
          With sudden blow—
Misfortune mark'd thee for her prey,
          And laid thee low.

TO A BUTTERCUP.

Perchance some happy child at play,
Releas'd from pedagogic sway,
Came with his noisy comrades gay,
    A frolic band,
And tore thee from thy home away
    With reckless hand.

Type art thou of some luckless bard,
Who labours manfully and hard
To win Dame Fortune's kind regard,
    Then sees life's game
Close e'er he play his winning card
    For deathless fame.

Ah! sadly dost thou illustrate,
Poor flower, in thy hapless fate,
The frailty of this mortal state—
    Life's slender thread—
This isthmus that doth separate
    Us from the dead.

Flower, from thy doom we learn that we,
Sooner or later, fade like thee;
But all who tread unswervingly
    Fair Wisdom's way,
Are blessed, let the stern decree
    Come when it may.

'TIS BETTER ON BEFORE.

O ye who tread life's pilgrim away
 With weary heart and sore,
Find hope and comfort in the thought—
 'Tis better on before.

Though circumstances adverse be,
 And scanty be your store;
Be patient, brighter days will come;
 'Tis better on before.

'TIS BETTER ON BEFORE.

Though you may be beset by foes
　Who wound you o'er and o'er,
A crown awaits the victor's brow;
　'Tis better on before.

Ye struggling souls, who life's dark sky
　With anxious eyes explore,
List, as Hope whispers in your ear,
　'Tis better on before!

Though oft with gloomy fears oppress'd
　On this wild rocky shore,
"He giveth His beloved rest;"
　'Tis better on before.

What though we be of low estate,
　Of origin obscure,
Christ many mansions hath prepared;
　'Tis better on before.

Were this cold world our only rest,
　Unblest were we and poor;
This life is but a fleeting dream,
　'Tis better on before.

Though Ruin threaten our frail barque,
　And well nigh whelm it o'er,
We'll make the port of Heaven's deep calm:
　'Tis better on before.

What though friend after friend depart,
　And leave us lone and sore,
This life's a scene of constant change,
　'Tis better on before.

If langour's soft insidious touch
　This mortal frame steal o'er,
There is a land where none are sick,
　'Tis better on before.

Why should we mourn our lov'd ones gone
　As though all hope were o'er?
The saying's truth they sweetly prove—
　'Tis better on before.

There's not an ill this world contains
  That Heaven cannot cure,
Ye heirs of immortality,
  'Tis better on before !

The clouds that gather in life's sky
  And dim the prospect o'er,
Pierce with the eagle eye of faith !
  'Tis better on before.

Then come what may—earth's keenest woes—
  We'll dread them all no more ;
They but endure for a night,
  'Tis better on before.

A TRIBUTE.

(Lines written on hearing a bird singing in a Wood at Daybreak.)

SWEET bird, warbling all unseen,
  Hid within thy covert green
From intruding mortal eye,
Hymning the awakening sky,
Pouring forth serenely gay
Thine unpremeditated lay
To welcome the approaching day
When the faint incipient flush
Of Aurora's rosy blush
Softly gilds the mountain's brow,
And tinges verdant vales below.
Pretty feathered troubadour,
Opening thy melodious store
Of Heav'n-given minstrel lore ;
Making vocal the still wood
With thy melody's full flood.
Thou merry-hearted forester,

A TRIBUTE.

Dame Nature's willing chorister;
Awaken'd by thy tuneful voice,
The daisy opes its yellow eye;
For joy the gentle breezes sigh,
The lovely flowerets rejoice,
And bashfully uplift their heads
From their dew-bespangl'd beds,
To listen to thy matin song—
A beauteous sympathetic throng.
Bright Phœbus, as he strides along,
Like mail-clad warrior bold and strong
With warm approval lists thy lays,
And generously largesse flings,
In golden glints on thy soft wings,
And thus thy tuneful toils repays.
Thou tiny soul of joy and glee,
Fluttering with ecstacy,
Making known with rapturous zest,
The joy that animates thy breast —
Teeming with a sweet unrest.
I love thy tender simple strain,
Strong antidote to care and pain;
Sweeter to me thy artless trill
By far than train'd artistic skill,
Where ofttimes affectation's art
Plays so conspicuous a part.
Sing on, dear bird. pour forth at will,
His praise Who gave thee thy sweet skill;
Contribute thou right lavishly
Thy share in Nature's minstrelsy;
Mingle thou thy pure refrain
With the universal strain
That through Creation's wide domain
Rolls on in volume rich and grand,
O'er azure sea, o'er smiling land,
Till blends it with the ceaseless song
Of yonder blest angelic throng,
While countless ages roll along.

NORA DOONE.

I FONDLY lov'd a maiden fair,
   I liv'd but in her eyes,
And all the mundane scene for me
   Contain'd no dearer prize ;
While some crav'd wealth, and rank, and power,
   I ask'd no richer boon
Of Fortune than to win the heart
   Of lovely Nora Doone.

I won her heart ; Love's flowery path
   I trod with footsteps light,
And deem'd not that my beauteous day
   Could ever know a night ;
But from my lip the nectar cup
   Was dash'd and shatter'd soon ;
For envious Death tore from my arms
   My lovely Nora Doone.

Ye little birds, lament with me !
   Ye streams that glide along !
Ye restless plaintive breezes, swell
   The melancholy song !
My hopes like dead leaves thickly lie
   By Autumn's breezes strewn ;
And Life presents no charm for me
   Since 'reft of Nora Doone.

AN OLD OLD STORY.

IN a squalid London attic,
   By a candle's flick'ring light
Sits a weary woman sewing,
   Toiling far into the night ;
Grief and want have left their impress
   On her figure slim and weak,
And a fatal tinge of crimson
   Mantles her once rounded cheek.

AN OLD OLD STORY.

In her face the ling'ring traces
    Of a beauty wondrous rare
May be seen amid the ravage
    Sorrow has effected there ;
Now, her eyes, once mildly lustrous,
    Gleam unnaturally bright,
And her hair's dishevelled tresses
    Fall upon her shoulders slight.

Once she was a happy maiden—
    Source of ever new delight
Unto fond indulgent parents—
    Of her home the joy, the light ;
Petted darling of the village,
    Pride of all the country side,
In her innocence and beauty
    Happiness personified.

How her honest rural lovers
    Sought for and did fondly prize
As a treasure rich and precious
    One kind glance from her bright eyes ;
At her mandate roam'd the forest,
    Cull'd for her the fresh wild flowers,
Deem'd the hours spent in her service
    Brightest happiest of hours !

But, like bird of evil omen,
    To that peaceful village came
A gay votary of fashion—
    Bearer of a lofty name—
Came he with his polished manners
    This poor maiden to ensnare,
Lure her from the path of virtue,
    Wreck her life so young and fair.

Ah ! that fatal ill-starr'd meeting—
    Memory's regretful glance
Often brings the scene before her—
    The rural fete, festive dance ;
The hastily sought introduction,
    And the stranger's ardent gaze,
Honey'd words of adulation,
    Fascinating winning ways.

AN OLD OLD STORY.

Then the frequent secret meeting—
    Fond embrace, impassioned kiss—
Solemn vows of true affection—
    Her sweet dream of coming bliss—
Conflict between love and duty—
    Dark temptation—hasty flight
From the dear parental homestead
    Under cover of the night.

'Tis, alas! the old, old story—
    Woman's trust, man's treachery—
Story but too oft repeated
    In the world's dark history;
O the bitter disenchantment—
    Waking from a vision fair,
But to find hopes fondly cherish'd
    Vanish'd into empty air!

Now alone, betray'd, deserted,
    All her beauty's brilliant bloom
Faded as a lovely flower
    Blighted in autumnal gloom;
Life denuded of its brightness—
    Nought her broken heart doth crave
But to rest from earthly sorrow
    In the quiet of the grave.

So the poor soul sits and labours,
    Slowly drooping day by day,
Sinking 'neath her heavy burden,
    Stranded on Life's ocean way;
God of Mercy, save and pardon
    This frail victim of deceit;
Draw her by Thy loving Spirit,
    Lead her gently to Thy feet!

Teach her, O all-pitying Saviour,
    Thou did'st come to save the lost—
Thou Who purchased Mankind's pardon
    At Thy life's infinite cost;
Guide her through death's darksome valley
    To the haven of the blest,
"Where the wicked cease from troubling
    And the weary are at rest."

CARPE DIEM.

PLUCK the lovely crimson rose,
  While its beauty brightly glows:
Ere the wind with angry gust
Trail its petals in the dust.

On yon azure-mantl'd sky,
Gladly feast the eager eye;
Ere the sombre storm-clouds gather,
And there cometh stormy weather.

Soon will yonder golden sun
His diurnal course have run;
Swiftly he his zenith wins,
Swiftly his decline begins.

List to Pleasure's dulcet lute,
Ere it lieth broken, mute,
And deep dirges of despair
Swell upon the saddened air.

Tender lovers, while ye may,
Wander through Love's flowery way:
Age, arrayed in cold and gloom,
Soon will steal your youthful bloom.

Labour's hardy children, seize,
Treasure each sweet spell of ease;
Duty's summons loud and clear,
Soon will sound upon your ear.

Of no future fondly dream,
Tinted by Hope's solar beam;
But the present be our care,
Let us make it bright and fair.

If to-day be calm and fair,
Who would be a prey to care?
Take no thought about to-morrow,
Courage from the present borrow.

Thus, with spirits stout and brave,
Sail we o'er life's restless wave;
Eating what the Gods provide,
Happy, whatso'er betide.

THE PEOPLE'S PARK.

*(Through the generosity of the late Sir Francis Crossley, Bart., M.P.,
presented to the Corporation of Halifax, and opened on the
14th of August, in the year 1857.)*

RESPLENDENT Muse, sweet spirit, deem'd by some
Of heavenly birth, to my assistance come!
Hail, loveliest thou of all the lovely Nine,
Whose peerless rays with dimless lustre shine!
Tutor'd by thee, O most benignant Maid,
Fain would I learn the poet's "tuneful trade;"
Vouchsafe to me the true Aeonian fire,
And boldly sweep my inartistic lyre;
Illume my soul with thy celestial spark
While I essay my theme—"The People's Park."

Three long decades have roll'd their circling way
Since that auspicious, memorable day,
When with eclat its gates were open thrown
Unto the people of our "good old town"—
Fair progeny of that munificence,
Which bless'd and blessing, widely did dispense
Its golden store without regard to creed,
Prompted alone by love of goodly deed.
Be ever praised that kindliness of heart
That fondly strove with Charity's soft art,
In harmony with heaven's noble plan,
To bless and cheer the changeful lot of man;
While throbs the heart, and memory holds its seat,
Shall gratitude the Crossley's praise repeat.

A pleasaunce fair, tho' of dimensions small,
A sweet boudoir in Nature's splendid hall,
Snugly enclos'd within a verdant square
Of arborets and foreign saplings rare;
A picturesque and beautiful retreat,
Yielding the studious eye refection sweet.
Trim well kept paths and lawny beds declare
With glad consent the gardener's lavish care;
And richly bright successively appear
The varying blooms that deck the floral year.
Pleasant its aspect when reviving Spring
Waves o'er the scene his wonder-working wing;
When surly Winter, growling with dismay,
His howling minions gruffly calls away;

And Flora comes the season fair to greet,
Laying her earliest offerings at his feet;
Beauteous when comes, child of yon glorious globe,
Gay Summer, in his many-coloured robe;
The skies put on their most superb array,
Their richest tints the flowers and trees display,
And like a thing of life the fountain gay
Tosses aloft bright showers of silvery spray.
The grass is dyed in deepest emerald green;
Refulgent Sol, presiding o'er the scene,
Illumines all with his unrivall'd shine;
Like burnish'd silver gleams the serpentine,
O'er whose clear face, with graceful arched throat,
The swan majestic tranquilly doth float,
While ducks respectful paddle in its wake,
Or eager rush to catch the floating "cake"—
As on the bridge delighted urchins stand,
Dispensing bounties with unstinting hand.
Pleasant it is in leisure hour to sit
As youth and beauty lightly by us flit,
On buoyant step, in healthful bloom array'd—
The sturdy youth, the modest, graceful maid—
Free from their toils in factory or mill,
Full of young hope, regardless of the ill
That may lie hidden in the future's haze,
Contented with the present's cloudless days.

   Nor shall the Muse disdain to notice here
That spot familiar, to our elders dear,
Which with the title proud, "Park Parliament,"
Is dignified by general consent;
Within whose quiet well-sheltered retreat,
Our aged sires, worn with the burden, heat
Of Life's stern fray, in solemn conclave meet;
Old cronies here each other warmly greet,
Here hold the frequent serious debate;
Here settle oft the great affairs of State,
Or fondly eulogise some hero great;
Tell of Time's changes, pleasures pass'd and gone,
The trials borne, the people they have known;
To Heav'n resigned, beguiling thus away
The closing hours of Life's declining day.

Still further aid me, Muse, while I regard
With thoughtful eye the spacious promenade—
The level terrace, graced on either side
With fragrant beds, the florist's special pride—
Bright dainty beauties, exquisitely choice,
Laid out in many an ingenious device ;
The massive cannon, frowning grimly down,
Stern witnesses of Albion's great renown,
Telling of noble actions nobly done,
Of daring deeds, and battles bravely won.
The grand pavilion, fittingly, I ween,
The central feature of the pleasant scene.
Ne shall the classic eye seek vainly for
The sculptor's art and mythologic lore ;
See Telemachus, victor from the fray,
Laying aside his militant array ;
Diana, beauteous Goddess of the Chase ;
The Dancing Girl, in attitude of grace ;
Great Hercules, the ancients' hero grand,
Firm as a rock in kingly pride doth stand ;
Apollo, Jove's illustrious progeny,
The God of Music, Science, Poetry ;
With Sophocles, the lustre of whose name
Won for Athenia everlasting fame ;
The Music Maiden with her tambourine ;
Unrivall'd Venus, Beauty's peerless Queen,
Lend dignity and finish to the scene.

When melancholy Autumn gazes down
Upon the prospect clad in russet brown ;
Tho' daylight shortens and the flowers are few,
And frequent teardrops Nature's cheek bedew ;
When leaves lie thickly on the humid ground,
While breezes sigh portentously around,
And Nature shrinks, as from impending harms ;
E'en then the scene hath its peculiar charms.
In all the seasons of the circling year—
In Spring's bright blush, or Winter's frown severe,
Rich gleams of Beauty's heavenly light appear.
Still, as Old Time goes on his busy round,
May our glad feet within the Park be found,
And may we have enlightened eyes to see

Fair Nature's gifts display'd so lavishly ;
And e'er may Heav'n smile brightly on our town,
Prosperity our labours richly crown ;
May we advance in all the arts of peace,
Our want diminish and our wealth increase ;
Upon us Knowledge bend her kindly glance,
May Science, Art, and Literature advance ;
And Halifax be never lost to fame
While we can boast the Crossley's honour'd name !

AT HOME.

A FISHER lad puts out to sea ;
    The breeze is whistling merrily,
His blue eye beams with love's soft light ;
His true love waves her kerchief white
Till o'er the wide expanse of blue
His boat fades swiftly from her view ;
While he sings, as he cuts the snowy foam,
" To-morrow will see me safe at home."

The maiden looks on the angry sea,
The billows leap tumultuously ;
Dark clouds on the wind's strong pinions fly,
Red lightening cleaves the ebon sky ;
The thunder's verberating roll
With terror fills the maiden's soul—
She prays, as her eyes o'er the dread scene roam,
" O that morning were here and my love at home."

Gray morning dawns on the treach'rous sea,
Smiling in cruel placidity ;
The bright sun darts his glances warm
On the beach, where lies a lifeless form ;
And bending beside it a weeping maid—
All life and hope from her bosom fled ;
No more to her arms her love will come,
For the fisher lad is safe at home.

NATURE'S SCHOOL.

ALL ye who would enrich your mind
With knowledge of the deepest kind,
Should seek it in fair Nature's school;
Beneath her kindly gentle rule,
No mind so barren, warp'd, or dull,
But from her open page may cull
Instruction of the highest worth.
No boundaries of caste or birth
Are recognised in her bright hall;
Her hand impartial levels all
The fine distinctions of mankind.
She but requires the pensive mind,
Encompass'd in patrician frame,
Or in a mould of lowlier name.
The son of toil's as welcome here
As is the offspring of a peer.
Wide open stands her college door
To great and small, to rich and poor;
The treasures of her beauteous lore
She in her volume grand displays,
And blest are they who spend their days
Amid her soul-entrancing sights,
Tasting her exquisite delights—
The flowers with their varying hues;
The heavens with their wondrous views;
Majestic Ocean's azure face;
The golden sun's unrivall'd rays;
The tender moon in softer sheen
Enfolding Evening's peaceful scene;
The myriads of lustrous stars
Careering in their silvery cars;
The lofty mountains, giant trees.
Deep tranquil valleys, greeny leas,
And songsters' thrilling minstrelries.
Uniting all in one bright plan,
With sweet accord they speak to man—
Incentives noble they present
And use the strongest argument
To wean him from each low pursuit

That tends but to degrade, embrute.
My brothers, all these voices hear ;
Whatever be your status, sphere—
Noble or simple, sage or fool,
Enrol yourselves in Nature's school.

THE SNOW.

THE angry northern winds do blow,
    And borne upon their pinions light,
    Whirling in fantastic flight,
Descends the powder'd silvery snow.

Swiftly the wold and towering height,
    Field, meadow, undulating dale
    Are cover'd with a beauteous veil,
Shimmering like silver bright.

How gay the landscape doth appear,
    Drap'd in its fairy-like array ;
    The icicles on hedge and spray
Sparkling like jewels, coldly clear !

A wondrous artist is the wind,
    Working at random his mad will,
    Portraying with unstudied skill
Pictures that charm the pensive mind.

Dame Nature, in her wintry garb,
    Festoon'd with spotless, downy wreath,
    Is beauteous, tho' her icy breath
Pierceth one like a pointed barb.

Art baffl'd views the splendid scene,
    Her highest powers inadequate
    Such pictures to delineate ;
Poorly she imitates, I wean

With years of labour hard and slow
    The fairy views superbly bright
    Created in a single night
By the wild vagaries of the snow.

SPEAK THE TRUTH.

SPEAK the truth ! Tho' the act
    Cost thee dear ;
Have nothing to regard, retract,
    Nought to fear.

Speak the truth ! Whatso'er
    Be at stake ;
Straight step over Virtue's fair
    Pathway take.

Speak the truth ! Let its rays
    Brightly shine ;
Be it clothed in homely phrase,
    Or in fine.

Speak the truth ! At any price
    Hold it fast ;
Heav'n will reward your sacrifice
    At the last.

Speak the truth ! 'Tis a gem
    Brighter far
Than stones in royal diadem,
    Or a star.

Speak the truth ! Stars shall fade,
    Gems decay ;
Truth, in dimless sheen array'd,
    Shines for aye.

Speak the truth ! Fear not man,
    Tho' he rave ;
Tho' thou'rt weak, Jehovah can
    Make thee brave.

Speak the truth ! For its sake
    Men have died ;
Their souls have risen from the stake
    Glorified.

Speak the truth ! Not in wrath,
    But in love ;
That tempted souls from Sin's dark path
    Ye may move.

Speak the truth! In youth, or age
　Falsehood flee;
Against it fiercest warfare wage
　Incessantly.

Speak the truth! When is pass'd
　Life's brief day,
The God of Truth will at the last
　Be your stay.

THE POWER OF KINDNESS.

DEEP down in every human heart,
　Within some secret cell,
However crush'd by sin and woe,
　Sweet chords of music dwell—
Which rise and fall in cadence grand
When waken'd by Love's gentle hand.

No soul, however vile and dark,
　Wherein we may not trace
Some flickerings of the " vital spark "
　Of purity and grace;
None so debas'd but in them shine
Some beamings of the light divine.

A kindly word, a deed of love,
　Tears shed in sympathy,
The hardest heart may melt and move,
　Where cold austerity
Tends but to harden and repel;
Nought can resist Love's gentle will.

Yes, Love's a sweet a beauteous gift
　By God Himself bestow'd
On finite men, their hearts to lift
　To Heaven—Love's bright abode;
And he who loves his fellow-man
Best carries out Jehovah's plan.

THE SOLO BOY.

(Dedicated to Walter Crawshaw, of this town, who was solo boy at the Parish Church at the time the poem was written.)

HE sits within the carven stall—
　The *dux* of all the songsters small,
In surplice white, and muslin collar,
Denoting him the music scholar;
With leadership and pride of place
Writ large upon his rosy face.
About him are the lesser fry,
Gazing with proud and envious eye
On their young chieftain in his seat,
Each wishing he'd a voice as sweet
And strong as his; for well know they
Whate'er the service for the day—
Roberts in F, Garland in A—
His voice rings out distinctly clear
Above his very best compeer.
Free, as the lark on heavenward wings,
His varying notes the youngster sings;
The music of each sacred strain
Floats through the venerable fane;
His song takes hold of many a heart
And oft th' unbidden tear will start—
Meet tribute to the singer's art.
The congregation know him well,
And love his triumphs oft to tell.
Ah! happy singer, well for thee
Could these bright days for ever be,
And thou a star serenely shine
In music's firmament divine.

Alas! on Time's fleet pinions borne,
There dawns a fatal Sabbath morn,
That dims, as clouds a summer sky,
The lustre of the solo boy.
He manages the Psalms all right,
The service sings with all his might;
But, as the anthem goes along,
The singers feel there's something wrong;
His voice, erstwhile so strong and clear,

Is weak and quav'ring as with fear;
Then, as he struggles on his way,
The youngsters hear with dire dismay
Their luckless leader crack on A.
O how by words shall be express'd
The pain that fills his boyish breast,
As, shrinking from the *maestro's* eye,
He heaveth many a bitter sigh,
And feels and knows, with bosom sore,
His solo days are almost o'er!

Grieve not too much, dear solo boy,
The closing of thy day of joy.
We in proverbial parlance say
That every dog but has its day.
Decay and failure wait on all
Who tread this roving mundane ball.
The flowers wear their fair array
But for a transitory day;
The fleetest racer on the track
Becomes some day the jaded hack;
The belle that sets all hearts aflame
The wither'd, worn, decrepit dame;
The batsman plays his brilliant game;
Time flies, and he is but a name.
Sweet singer, well you've played your part
In the sublime celestial art;
And, having done your very best,
You now must give way like the rest.

Then chorister, despond no more;
Who knows what Fate may have in store?
As time goes on perchance you'll find
Dame Nature will again be kind,
And unto thee the power impart
To labour in the beauteous art;
Perhaps the vaulted aisle again
May echo to your ringing strain.
But if not, then " fond Memory "
Will prove a faithful friend to thee;
She oft will pour into thine ears
The music of these earlier years;

Oft to thy tear-dimm'd eyes recall
The dear familiar choir-stall.
In fancy, wearing with delight
The surplice and the collar white,
Thus shall you live again with joy
The days when you were solo boy.

A LITERARY TRAGEDY.
In Three Acts. (After Gilbert.)
Act 1.

AN editor sits in a dingy old den, his shining scissors near
His good right hand, and a "Devil's Own" pen in his editorial ear;
With a stony stare and a brow of care he toils assiduously;
Not a moment must stop he, for waiting for "copy," six hungry "comps" there be;
'Twas a pleasant sight to watch him write with a hand so light and free;
It did me good, as there I stood, to see such industry.

Act 2.

Now a rhyming rip, with a stealthy step, climbed softly up the stairs,
In his hand a book, he'd a weird wild look, and his clothing needed repairs.
He gazed at that slaving scribbling scribe with meek humility,
Then said he'd a poem he'd much like to show him—a gem of poesy;
And there I stood, in a pleasant mood, expecting soon to see
That office floor steeped in the gore of the man of poetry.

Act 3.

The editor gaz'd like one half craz'd, but ne'er a word spake he;
Then he gave a lurch, and slid from his perch with fierce alacrity;
He grabb'd that weird and wild-eyed bard and dragg'd him to the door;
Downstairs he shot him, from top to the bottom, and the rhymer was no more;
And the editor then sat down in his den and laugh'd with fiendish glee;
So, bards, beware! and avoid the lair of the man of industry.

A NOVEMBER DAY.

ALL Nature's rob'd in gloom to-day,
    Above, below, around;
The sun witholds his golden ray;
    Upon the humid ground

In sodden'd clusters lie the leaves,
    The heavens darkly frown,
And freely from the dripping eaves
    The rain drops patter down.

The bird upon the leafless tree
    No silvery pæan sings,
But droops in dull despondency
    Its saturated wings.

The spectral trees unto the sky
    Uplift their naked arms,
The restless breezes moan and sigh;
    Denuded of their charms

Fair Flora's rifl'd bowers stand,
    And vapours thickly rise,
Until it seems as if the land
    Were blended with the skies.

A dense impenetrable gloom
    Rules over all the scene,
Enfolding as within a tomb
    The daylight's cheery sheen.

Yet doth this dismal, gloomy scene—
    This dark November day,
A useful lesson teach, I wean—
    To me it seems to say:

The way to happiness and light
    Oft lies through sorrow's gloom;
There must be winter's withering blight
    Before the spring's bright bloom.

Be patient; yet a little while,
  My aspect cold and grey
Must give place to the sunny smile
  Of happy blithesome May.

Then let us patiently abide
  Stern winter's circling gloom,
Until again, in spring's sweet tide,
  The lovely flowers bloom.

THE MERMAIDS.

DEEP fathoms 'neath the restless sea,
  In many a beauteous cell,
Embosom'd in tranquility
  The lovely mermaids dwell;
Laving in Neptune's current gold
Their shapely forms and heads of gold.
Where pinky coral gaily gleams
  And pearls like rainbows shine—
Their lustre rivalling the beams
  Of jewels of the mine;
And grows full many a strange sea flower,
Is the mermaids' hidden fairy bower.

They are the syrens of the sea
  Who smile but to destroy,
As winsomely, seductively,
  By wile and art they try
To lure the mariner to his doom
And shroud his form in a watery tomb.

When the favouring currents flow
  All placidly along,
With Pleasure seated at the prow
  Their heart with courage strong;
Go Neptune's gallant offspring true,
The wearers of the jacket blue.

Ah, thoughtless mariner, beware!
  These houri of the sea,
With winning smile and tresses fair,
  They bode no good for thee;
For, like their land-born sisters, they
Regard thee as their natural prey.

ROBERT BURNS.

ONE day I saw a picture fair that fill'd me with delight,
It represented Poetry, in flowing robes of white,
Her brow adorn'd with classic bays, her harp slung by her side,
Throwing her mantle over Burns, auld Scotia's joy and pride.
There stood the honest ploughman in homely garb array'd,
His bonnet doff'd right courteously before the lovely maid,
And near beside him was the plough behind whose iron share
In loneliness oft plodded the deathless " Bard of Ayr "—
That glittering constellation in the firmament of fame,
A "gifted peasant" destin'd to immortalize his name
And bequeath unto posterity a legacy of song,
An untold wealth of melody, rich, bountiful, and strong.

I gaz'd upon the picture, until lost in reverie quite,
Methought the senseless canvas seem'd aglow with living light,
Teeming with objects beautiful array'd in brilliant beams,
Hills, dales, and flowery valleys, green meadows, silvery streams—
The food and inspiration of the poet's varied themes.
Then pass'd before my vision in grotesque fantastic train
The marvellous creations of his busy, facile brain.
First, immortal " Tam O Shanter," as on that dreadful night,
When mounted on his " gude auld mare " he urg'd his headlong
    flight
Past Alloway's " auld ruin'd Kirk," athrough the storm and dark,
Pursued by imps and warlocks, led by lissome " Cutty Sark."
I saw him gain the " key-stane " by " gude Maggie's " gallant
    jump,
Heard the fiendish yell of triumph as " Nannie " by the rump
Fast gripp'd the luckless mare and rove her tail out by the stump.
I overheard the dialogue between the " Brigs o' Ayr,"
As they in altercation past and present did compare ;
I noted the " Twa Dogs " as in converse grave and gay
They discoursed upon the customs, follies, fashions of the day.
And then methought I view'd with inexpressible delight
The tender scenes depicted in the " Cottar's Saturday Night ; "
I saw the humble toiler beside his ingle bright,
His children's ruddy faces illum'd with Love's soft light,
As for a transient season he lays aside his care—
In his dear lov'd ones' pleasures with youthful heart to share ;
I heard the grand old psalm tune swell on the stilly air,

Mark'd the patriot and saint as he breath'd the fervent prayer
That heaven would guard " auld Scotland " with a peculiar care.
Then all the scene was chang'd, and I marked the noisy glee
Of Willie, Rob, and Allan, the boon companions three,
The lads that " were na fou, but just a drappie i' their ee ;"
Saw the poet in the field bending o'er the startled mouse ;
Mark'd him sitting in the Kirk as he gravely watched a louse
Marching in and out the trimmings of a lady's Sunday bonnet—
Heard his chuckle of delight as he penn'd his verses on it ;
In fancy almost caught the pathetic " fare thee weel "
With which the bard concluded his " Address unto the Deil ;"
Then heard that plaintive dirge—of pain and sorrow borne,
As the anguish-stricken poet told how " Man was made to Mourn,"
When he saw with tearful eye " Man's inhumanity to man "
To discord change the harmony of Nature's noble plan ;
Last, I stood within his cottage when, as he sat alone,
The Muse again appeared to him and claim'd him as her own,
And o'er his soaring soul diffus'd her spirit-stirring fire,
Tuning to noble lofty flights his untaught rustic lyre,
Bidding him climb with steadfast step the steep ascent of fame,
And gild his country's annals with the lustre of his name.

Then waking from my reverie, I thought with deep regard
On the virtues of this wondrous and incomparable bard ;
His lofty-soul'd disdain for the soulless venal tribe
Who prostitute their genius for place or filthy bribe ;
His stern incisive censure of national misdeeds,
His heartfelt deep aversion to lifeless forms and creeds,
And patriotic pleadings of his lov'd Scotland's needs ;
His hatred of injustice, inherent sense of right,
Fierce scorn for all oppressors and willingness to fight
In freedom's holy battle, his grand superb disdain
For all who us'd Religion for purposes of gain ;
That sturdy independence that fain would suffer want
Than cringe before Earth's great ones and play the sycophant.

And on his many errors I look'd with lenient eye
As I thought of his sad story—how much there was to try
A being so impulsive, so prone to go astray
And let his baser passions his nobler nature sway.
Then I thought with deepest pleasure of the good his songs have
    done,

The comfort and the blessing they have been to many a one;
How many a drooping spirit held down by grief and pain
Hath been help'd along Life's journey by the music of his strain.
How those songs retain their sweetness, their elevating power,
Still exercise their influence in sad or festive hour,
Still wield with subtle magic their soul subduing art,
Filling with pride and pleasure each true-born Scottish heart;
And those glorious masterpieces so lofty and sublime
Shall shine in dimless splendour upon the scroll of time,
Like flowers amaranthine and beautiful for aye,
Imperishable monuments triumphant o'er decay;
For while this wand'ring planet on her axis daily turns
Shall endure the glorious memory and songs of Robert Burns.

A TRUE MAN.

I love the man who loves his kind;
  The man whose comprehensive mind
No boundaries knows of caste or creed.
Who ever at the cry of need
Will bend a sympathetic ear;
Whose constant spirit will not veer
About life shifting weather-vane;
But true and faithful will remain
Through weal or woe beside his friend,
His worth and goodness know no end;
He cannot witness mortal pain
Without an effort to restrain
Pity's involuntary tear.
He, when is pour'd into his ear
Some moving tale of human woe,
Can ever feel the generous glow
Of Charity's ennobling flame.
This is a man for whom I claim
The highest praise, the best regard—
The true man's well-deserv'd reward—
This is the manhood I commend;
Kind Heav'n! Provide me such a friend,
Him to my soul I'll tightly clasp,
And nought but Death shall loose my grasp.

THE FOREST.

I LOVE the forest's still retreat—
　Far from the city's hum—
No worldly tumults come
To mar the happiness complete;
Here Solitude her peaceful throne
Hath set, and reigns supreme, alone.

'Tis sweet to sit in thoughtful mood
　In eve's calm hour,
　'Neath Fancy's power;
As memories sweet—a holy brood—
Like visions bright before us rise,
Then fade from our regretful eyes.

I love to tread the sylvan glade
　And pensively explore
　Its verdant velvet floor,
By Flora's busy hand array'd
In robe of deeply-tinted green,
Where many a starry flower is seen.

Nobles may boast their mansions fair,
　Where cunning art
　Plays its bright part;
Where painting rich and carving rare,
Chaste Statuary, gilded sheen,
Conspire to beautify the scene.

But give me Nature's pure demesnes,
　Sweet fairy bowers
　Bedeck'd with flowers,
Made vocal with the thrilling strains
Of songsters warbling joyously;
O this is pleasure rich to me!

What power in this stillness dwell!
　No noisy throes
　Of striving foes;
O forest! to thy peaceful cells
Oft would my joyful steps repair,
And snatch a rest from worldly care.

THE REPRIEVE.

THE deep boom of the castle bell
    Reverberates o'er hill and dell,
Sounding a mortal's dying knell.
    Miserere Domine!

The pris'ner in his donjon cell
Hears the deep tone of that sad bell;
Its summons stern he knows full well.
    Miserere Domine!

O woeful sight for mortal eye,
A gallant youth led out to die;
Kind angels tend him from on high.
    Miserere Domine!

Between his guards with steady pace,
With form erect and fearless face,
He goes, the pride of his proud race.
    Miserere Domine!

The doomsman stands in grim array,
And hovering o'er those turrets grey,
Insatiate Death awaits his prey.
    Miserere Domine!

His aged mother, too, is there,
With bending form and snowy hair,
Breathing on high the tremulous prayer.
    Miserere Domine!

The teardrops lave his limpid eye,
His bosom heaves a long, deep sigh,
As to his love his fond thoughts fly.
    Miserere Domine!

The kind confessor tends him there,
An aged priest with brow of care,
With solemn rite and holy prayer.
    Miserere Domine!

That dauntless soul that, like a rock,
Had stood mid battle's fiercest shock,
Approaches now the fatal block.
    Miserere Domine!

But hark! a murmur passes round;
Is clearly heard the clattering sound
Of horse hoofs beating the hard ground.
   Miserere Domine!

Dashing along at lightning speed,
A courier urges his brave steed;
Shouting aloud he bids them heed.
   Miserere Domine!

On, courier, on! Each sinew strain.
On, gallant horse! The courtyard gain
Ere the red stream the stone floor stain.
   Miserere Domine!

A moment, and upon the scene,
The pris'ner and his doom between,
They stand with pardon from the Queen.
   Gloria tibi Domine!

O rapture! bliss without alloy,
What words can tell the maiden's joy,
Or mother's, as she clasps her boy?
   Gloria tibi Domine!

To Heav'n, Who intervened that day,
The headsman's horrid hand to stay,
Ascends the glad triumphant lay—
   Gloria tibi Domine!

MY LITTLE BOY WHO DIED.

OFT o'er my mind a sweet sad thought
   Will come in pensive hour—
A tender recollection fraught
   With deep mysterious power;
And then my fancy seems to see
   A bright form by my side—
Smiling with fond delight on me—
   My little boy who died.

MY LITTLE BOY WHO DIED.

Tho' many years their course have sped
   Since the dark angel came
Into our home on errand dread—
   Our darling one to claim;
The soft unbidden tear will fall,
   My weakness who shall chide
As memory fondly doth recall
   My little boy who died?

I see again the fair green field
   We roam'd with busy feet,
The butterfly that whirling wheel'd
   The summer flowers sweet.
O fairer prospects now he views
   Than earthly scenes supplied;
He roams mid flowers of fadeless hues,
   My little boy who died!

Ah! sacred is that little drawer,
   Embalm'd with many a sigh,
Where, dearer far than pearly store,
   Our darling's treasures lie—
Drum, trumpet, lamb with fleece of snow,
   Top, soldiers side by side—
Dear trifles that delighted so
   My little boy who died.

Tho' other little pattering feet
   To meet me run with glee;
And other little voices sweet
   Make merry minstrelsie;
Yet still there mingles with my joy
   A grief I cannot hide—
The thought of that dear little boy—
   My little one who died.

And oft a tender, silvery voice
   Seems speaking from the sky,
Saying:— "My mother dear, rejoice!
   The time is drawing nigh
When we shall meet;" then calmly still
   In patience I abide;
Until I join when 'tis God's will
   My little boy who died.

GUARDIAN ANGELS.

GUARDIAN Angels, beings beauteous,
   Quitting oft their blissful bowers,
Unto heavenly mandate duteous,
   Visiting this realm of ours;
God's delighted, willing minions,
   Serving in His temple bright,
Bearing to these dark dominions
   Blessings on their pinions white.

Hovering o'er some lowly dwelling,
   Comforting the troubled heart;
When the storms of life are swelling
   Hope and courage they impart;
Spreading the inspiring vision
   Oft before our tearful eyes—
Glimpses bright of fields Elysian—
   Golden streets of Paradise.

Oft in faithful vigil bending
   O'er the bed of innocence,
From all evil dreams defending;
   Unto faith and penitence
Harden'd sinners gently gaining,
   Guiding the rash steps of youth,
Tempted ones from ill restraining,
   Winning them to Wisdom, Truth.

Beauteous Spirits, watching o'er us
   As we tread this earthly maze,
Lighting up the way before us,
   Guiding through Life's devious ways,
Whispering your sweet evangels,
   Fainting hearts to bless and cheer;
Stay with us, kind Guardian Angels,
   Till earth's clouds shall disappear!

A BIRTHDAY WISH.

MAY each recurring natal day
   Find you pursuing Wisdom's way;
Treading with firmer steps the road
That leads to happiness and God.

TO GENERAL GORDON.

GREAT Gordon, lion-hearted soul.
Saint, hero, true philanthropist,
Thou type of highest chivalry!
Who can recall thy hapless doom—
The tale of thy untimely fate
Unmov'd, nor shed soft Pity's tear?
Now numbered with the holy dead,
All undisturb'd by earth's alarms,
The fragrance of thy pure grand life
Remains with us who mourn thy loss.
Ill can we spare such men as thee;
The roll of our illustrious dead
Contains no brighter name than thine.
While Memory's faculty remains
With each true son of Albion,
The splendid lessons thou hast taught—
Thy manly Spartan fortitude,
And sense of duty strong and high,
Thy perfect disregard of self,
Insensibility to fear;
Thy tender, ceaseless sympathy
With all the sorrows of thy race,
And never-failing interest
In every object tending to
The elevation of mankind
Can never be forgot. Again
We feel the burden of suspense
That weighed our anxious nation down,
When in the hour of urgent need,
Responsive unto Duty's call,
Thou sped'st upon thy lonely way
Athwart the Desert's arid waste
To aid the helpless Soudanese
Against the Mahdi's phrenzied hordes.
And how for twelve dark weary months
With patient courage thou did'st wait
That look'd-for succour which, alas!
Thou wert not destined to behold.
Then came that memorable hour
When Treachery's infernal arts
Accomplish'd that which force of arms

Had vainly striven to achieve—
When pour'd through Khartoum's massive gates
Like surging waves the ruthless foe—
Who, senseless to thy priceless worth,
Unmov'd by Pity's softening power,
Upon thee fell with coward force
And blotted out thy glorious life.
Ah, then what tears of bitter woe
Our stricken sorrowing nation shed,
And men all felt that from their midst
Had pass'd one of the grandest souls
That e'er inhabited the frame
Of man. Rest, gallant warrior, rest ;
No more o'er thy intrepid heart
Shall earthly tempests fiercely beat ;
No more shall cold indifference
Ere wound thy earnest fervent breast.
And if the lessons thou hast taught,
By Memory's impressive power
Be deeply graven in our minds,
And others of Britannia's sons
Thy lofty actions emulate,
Not vainly hast thou liv'd and died.

A POLITICAL BALLAD.

THE Grand Old Man to the war hath gone,
 At St. Stephen's you will find him,
His grand old axe he hath girded on,
 And his Homer slung behind him ;
Upas tree, cries the G.O.M.,
 Tho' all the Tories praise thee,
I'll hack thee branch, and root, and stem,
 And to the ground I'll raze thee.

Greater than Dilke or Chamberlain
 I've made a name in story ;
I treat with most superb disdain
 The ilk that's christened Tory.
No Churchill's tongue shall flurry me
 With dire threats of exposure ;
I'll drown him in verbosity
 And crush him with the Closure !

PLEASURES.

ALAS! the fairest, sweetest flowers
    Wear their beautiful array
But for transitory hours
    E'er they yield unto decay.

Pleasures are like fading flowers,
    Flitting gleams of golden light,
Swift as meteoric showers,
    Gone ere you can mark their flight.

Robber Time, with ruthless fingers,
    Dims the eye and lines the cheek,
Till of beauty's light there lingers
    But a faint a shadowy streak.

Still the heart doth fondly cherish—
    Treasure up the precious rays;
Memory will not let them perish,
    The sweet joys of bygone days.

THO' FAR FROM THEE.

THO' far from thee, dear maid, I rove,
    Ah! think not I can faithless prove;
Where'er I roam no sun can shine
Upon a dearer face than thine;
The brightest day is but as night
Unless thou'rt near to bless my sight—
Bereft of thee, my light of light,
    Life hath no charms for me.

Can I forget thee? Aye, as soon
As yonder mellow-visag'd moon
Can cease to shed her silvery beam
On tranquil wood and slumbering stream.
Where'er I be, on ocean main,
Or on some distant foreign plain,
In fancy sweet again, again,
    I'll feast my eyes on thee.

THE FIRST KISS.

LET poets sensuous combine
　　To rave about their ruby wine;
With fulsome phrase let them extol
The pleasures of the flowing bowl;
I sing a far serener joy—
Pure gold unmingled with alloy;
The nectar rich of earthly bliss—
That lovers taste—the first sweet kiss.

Yon miser in his dingy den
Go mark as o'er and o'er again
He counts with wildly gleaming eyes
His shining hoard that outspread lies;
His sun and centre sordid self;
His *summum bonum* filthy pelf;
How mean, how poor a joy is his
Compared with love's first tender kiss!

That pensive student as he toils
To wrest from Learning her fair spoils
While all the world is wrapp'd in sleep;
His inward glow of rapture deep
As he discerns from Nature's page
Some lesson hid from bearded sage,
Ill rivals the delicious bliss
Of love's impassioned sweet first kiss.

Then let the poets have their wine
And loudly in its praise combine,
The wretched miser feast his eyes
Upon his glitt'ring golden prize,
The student nightly o'er his page
Drink in the learning of his age;
I ask no sweeter joy than this—
The joy of joys, love's fond first kiss.

MAY AND DECEMBER.

A SHORT time ago in the papers 'twas seen
　　That an old man had wedded a maid of eighteen;
Like King David, may be, he requir'd a young lass
To revive him, while she wanted him for his brass.

AUTUMN.

SUMMER'S rich hues have died away,
   And mellow Autumn now is here ;
He comes his kindly part to play,
   And crown the circling year.

A crown of varied-tinted leaves
   Upon his jovial brow he wears ;
A priceless load of golden sheaves
   Within his arms he bears.

Season of mirth and fruitfulness,
   Bringing the husbandman's reward
For all his hopes, anxieties,
   His labours long and hard.

He comes with timely hand to grease
   The flagging wheels of Industry ;
To make them run with power and ease
   And work more evenly.

He opens Plenty's ample horn,
   And pours upon the heaving plain
Her luscious fruits—the generous corn,
   " Bright Ceres' golden rain."

The pleasant sounds of Harvest Home
   Ring blithely o'er the gladden'd plain,
As forth the merry reapers come
   In busy jocund train.

The skies are bath'd in mellow'd light,
   The fields are ting'd with sober brown ;
And with a lustre mildly bright,
   The harvest moon beams down.

O! with what powerful eloquence
   Doth Autumn's voice unto us preach,
And truths of deep significance
   In solemn accents teach.

He bids us mark the flower, the leaf,
   Clad in the garments of decay ;
And hear them breathe this sentence brief,
   Thou art but for a day.

He points out in the falling leaf
    Token of Death's prevailing power ;
And teaches in the full-eared sheaf
    The resurrection hour.

This world of ours is God's great field,
    Where we by thought and action sow
The pregnant mighty seeds that yield
    Eternal weal or woe.

So may we live and labour here,
    That we can view without dismay
The Harvest of the World draw near—
    The final reaping day.

PRACTICAL SYMPATHY.

"HOW sorry I am," you oft hear people say
    As they view the misfortunes of others,
But practical sympathy how few display
    To their indigent sisters and brothers ;
Protestations of pity *sans* generous aid
    Are worthless to persons in trouble—
Mere meaningless jargon, a hollow parade,
    As bodiless as a soap bubble.

This statement to illustrate, let me repeat
    A story I somewhere have read
Of the Merchant and Quaker who met in the street,
    When the former in confidence said :
Poor G——'s going down I hear on good grounds,
    I feel awfully sorry I vow ;
Quoth the Quaker : I *feel* five hundred good pounds
    In my pocket, Friend, how much dost thou ?

Merely telling the poor man who begs at your gate
    You feel very much for his woes
Will not help in the least his pangs to abate
    If away from you empty he goes ;
No; practical sympathy, that is the best,
    Kind Nature's akin-making touch ;
As is well by the old Latin proverb express'd,
    " He who promptly gives, gives twice as much."

TRUE NOBILITY.

CHILD of labour, don't repine
    That a lowly lot be thine;
Deem it not unmix'd misfortune
That toil, privation, are your portion.
Tho' your status be ignoble,
You may live a life right noble,
That shall dignify your state,
Make you really, truly great,
If with actions good and true,
You Life's journey way bestrew.
The man of honest, simple heart,
Daily playing well his part;
Does his work with single mind,
Sympathizes with his kind
In the hour of pain and grief;
Lends with ready hand relief,
Succours the distress'd, the poor,
Even from a scanty store;
Sheddeth Pity's melting tear
When is breath'd into his ear
Some sad narrative of woe;
Or displays the fiery glow
Of indignation on his cheek
When he sees the helpless weak
Bullied by the tyrant strong,
Or oppressed by fraud or wrong;
Who will whisper kind reproof
In the ear of thoughtless youth
When from Wisdom's pleasant way
Evil tempteth them to stray;
In short, who in a thousand ways
A lively interest displays
In all pertaining to his race:
I say in this man we can trace
The lines of true nobility,
Altho' no garter at his knee
Denote him one of high degree.
Yet still in Nature's kindly plan,
He is the genuine nobleman,
In Virtue's Aristocracy
Holding honourable degree.

THE VOICE OF THE "COMP."

'TIS the voice of the Comp, I hear him complain,
As he peers in the box : What, no copy again !
Not the ghost of a " par," not even an " ad " ;
It's enough to make even a clergyman mad.

To be kept idle thus is really hard " lines ;"
If I could I'd establish a system of fines,
So that whene'er the copy ran out, do you see,
The Reporters should stump up the sum of " 3d."

Later on in the day I hear him again,
This time 'tis the Reader that causes him pain :
He's the bane of my life, so frequently bringing
Me out of my " frame " through neglecting his " ringing."

Oft and oft in a week does he play me that trick ;
Sometimes as I'm cheerfully filling my " stick,"
Number——bawls the lad in imperative tone,
And I put up a prayer as I waltz round the stone,

But to find after all 'twas not in the copy,
And if in at that moment the Reader should pop, he
Would hear me in strong terms express my opinion ;
But he keeps out of sight the pen-driving " minion."

I think you will own 'tis a very hard " case "
To be, tho' no Nimrod, called out to the " chase,"
Especially just when I'm most anxious to be
In-scooping the " sheks." with a column of " ruby."

Tho' I lecture him on typographical " rule "
My technical teachings are lost on the fool ;
He listens with such an indifferent air,
I might just as well talk to my " clump " I declare.

I suppose I must just let him have his own way,
And bear with his awkwardness day after day,
Till I go to the land of the happy and blest
Where " Readers " cease troubling and " Comps." are at rest.

DESCENT IS EASY.

IN " facilis descensus est "
   There is a bitter truth expressed,
Which oft we see exemplified
In overthrow of pomp and pride ;
Some haughty son of high estate
Fell'd by a sudden blow of Fate,
As lightning cleaves the sturdy oak
With rapid overwhelming stroke.
Or like the meteor that flies
In vivid splendour through the skies ;
Awhile in transient brilliance flashes,
Then sinks o'erwhelm'd in smoke and ashes.
Or like the lovely fragile flower
That wears but for a fleeting hour
Its fragrant beautiful array,
Then yields to darkness and decay.
We see a man of wealth one day
Bowl tranquilly along Life's way
In Fortune's gilded chariot light,
Whose every prospect seems most bright ;
To him his lowlier fellows bow,
And, in their envy, wonder how
The Fates with such a partial hand
Deal out the good things of the land :
And why it seems ordain'd that they
Should have to labour day by day
With but a scant precarious pay.
But mark that lovely crimson rose,
As brilliantly its beauty glows,
Dewdrops on its petals slight
Glittering like diamonds bright
In the sun's refulgent light ;
Ravishing the charmèd eye
With its fair form and gorgeous dye :
Diffusing its aroma rare
Upon the balmy morning air.
Ah ! 'neath that beautiful array
Lurk envious Death and dire decay ;
For if we lift the tender leaf,
And gaze attentively beneath,

We see the hideous loathsome form
Of the destroying canker-worm.
And so it is with mortal man
Full often in Life's complex plan.
We see him in the festive hour,
Beneath the spell of Pleasure's power,
Assuming with most subtle art
A smiling face, the while his heart,
To some deep hidden grief a prey,
Consumeth gradually away.
Then envy not the rich and great—
The splendid sons of rank and state;
They have their sorrows and their cares,
Trials, innumerable snares.
The rather cast your eyes around
The little plot on Life's vast ground
In which is fix'd your lowlier fate,
And in it strive to cultivate
The peaceful fruits of Righteousness,
That yield nor strife nor bitterness;
But the sweet flowers of Virtue, Truth,
That bloom in amaranthine youth
When worldly pageant and display
In rusty splendour fade away.
Seek, seek to cultivate the mind;
Live, live to benefit your kind;
A noble life, a spotless name,
Are fairer far than empty fame.
To live in Virtue's whiteness dress'd
Is to be happy, to be bless'd.

THE SPECIAL CORRESPONDENT.

(Sung by Mr. C. Clucas in the Nautical Operetta, "Sons of Neptune.")

I'M a literary wonder—an independent scribe—
Who never makes a blunder, and never takes a bribe,
I've a *modus operandi* entirely my own,
As contributor to journals of a highly moral tone;
No human weakness ever gets the upperhand of me,
Encas'd in incorruptible impeccability;
For I'm the very soul of honour and Nature's nobleman,
The correspondent of the *Courier* and *Guardian*.

THE SPECIAL CORRESPONDENT.

Upon this roving planet I keep my Argus eyes,
And the doings of its people very closely scrutinize,
No little peccadillo, nor smallest circumstance
Of the trivialest nature eludes my vigilance ;
I do my level best to be thoroughly *au fait*
With everything transpiring around me day by day ;
To be on the *qui vive* ever is the literary plan
Of the correspondent of the *Courier* and *Guardian*.

I can analyse a dog fight with dialectic skill,
Describe in racy jargon the latest little "mill" ;
I give the truest prophecies in every branch of sport,
Or authentic information of the goings-on at Court ;
Abuse some budding author, criticise the newest play,
And dub it "awful rot" in my inimitable way ;
For a complete encyclopedia, a Protean-minded man
Is the correspondent of the *Courier* and *Guardian*.

Many a weighty mission I have been on in my time,
From the freezing frigid zone to the tropics' torrid clime ;
Oft on the rolling billows heard the tempests crack their throats,
Or on gigantic mountain tops I've jotted down my notes ;
Stood on the battlefield with cannon's fiery breath
All around about me belching forth red ruin, pain, and death ;
Of many a "campaign" have I closely watched the "plan,"
As correspondent of the *Courier* and *Guardian*.

Of the adventures of the "Neptune" just now it is my lot
In my eighteen carat form full particulars to jot ;
I affably converse with the communicative tars,
List the howling of the wind and pen my glowing "pars."
I paint attractive pictures of life upon the sea,
And rave about our nation's maritime supremacy,
In a style that demonstrates that I'm just the very man
As correspondent of the *Courier* and *Guardian*.

Tho' somewhat at a loss for naval phraseology,
Scarcely able to determine hard-a-port from hard-a-lee,
And tho' upon the average I'm sea-sick twice a day,
My time upon the whole passes pleasantly away ;
And when our foemen duly have been sent to Davy Jones,
And Peace again returning hushes Battle's blustering tones,
In the march of civilization still I'll occupy the van,
As correspondent of the *Courier* and *Guardian*.

"NEVER SAY DIE!"

O NEVER say die!
   In darkest hour,
Tho' over Life's sky
   The storm-clouds lour;
Tho' dreary be the path you tread,
And tempests gather overhead,
   Never say die.

O never say die!
   Tho' foes assail,
Tho' dark danger nigh
   The cheek may pale;
Without a friend to aid and cheer,
And not a ray of hope appear,
   Never say die!

O never say die!
   Resolve not to yield,
Nor, coward-like, fly
   From Life's battlefield;
Like true Britons fight till the last gasp of breath,
And no victor own but all-conquering Death.
   Never say die!

O never say die!
   The strife must cease,
And by and bye,
   Come rest and peace;
Pleasure's fair train in bright array,
And halcyon harmonious day;
   Never say die!

O never say die!
   Be patient, strong,
With hopes on high
   March straight along;
Until shall come the glorious day
When all Earth's clouds shall melt away;
   Never say die!

EVENING.

NOW dusky-visag'd Evening flings
  Her ebon-tinted circling wings
Athwart this scene of mundane things.

Low sinks the kingly orb of day,
Illuming with his dying ray
The lofty hill tops far away.

High mounted on his silvern car
Comes forth the beauteous evening star,
Shedding its radiance from afar.

Pale Phœbe climbs her lofty hill,
And to the assemblage fair and still
Announces her imperial will.

Foremost in her attendant train,
Careering o'er the ethereal plain,
Bold Charles directs his shining wain.

Stern Mars in armour dazzling bright,
Great soul of courage and of might,
Waveth his blood-red banner bright.

Orion's sparkling belt is seen,
The Pleiades in brilliant sheen,
Adding their lustre to the scene.

O'er meadow, copse, and silent wood,
And slumb'ring stream deep quietude,
Like peaceful dove, doth sweetly brood.

The lowing cattle slowly wind
Their homeward way, the honest hind
Trudging wearily behind.

Now chime sweet Memory's silver bells,
Bright Fancy weaves her magic spells,
As on the past the mind oft dwells.

Then come array'd in lustrous light
A train of pleasant memories bright,
And fade from our regretful sight.

That peaceful thatch-roof'd cottage, where,
Kneeling beside our mother's chair,
We breath'd the oft-repeated prayer.

That little picturesque retreat,
Our village home, its meadows sweet,
Its one long solitary street.

A father's face benign and sage,
Conning intent the Holy Page,
His form bow'd 'neath the weight of age.

With tear-dimm'd eye perchance we trace
A dear lov'd sister's kindly face,
The joy, the darling of the place.

That sailor brother's well-knit form
We see amid the raging storm,
And breathe the supplication warm,

That He Who holds both sea and land
Within the hollow of His hand
Will still the waves at His command

And guide the good ship o'er the sea,
Through billows leaping furiously,
To the haven where they fain would be.

These friends so constant, kind, and true,
From whose companionship we drew
Such pleasure, wistfully we view.

Kind, faithful hearts, the true, the brave,
Scatter'd about by Time's strong wave,
And many slumbering in the grave.

O come dear light of by-gone days,
And bend on us your cheering rays,
Oft 'mid the Present's gloomy haze.

Yes, come to us again, again,
Bringing sweet pleasure in your train,
Till rest we from Life's weary strain!

THE LAY OF THE LOST MINSTREL.

UPON the water-butt he stood
    To serenade his love;
A merry maid in mirthful mood
    Lay listening above;
And as he strumm'd his light guitar,
    And utter'd notes divine,
The cats chipp'd in from near and far,
    And the effect was fine.

He sang the first verse of his lay,
    The second did begin,
When lo! the blessed lid gave way,
    And he went flopping in;
Beneath the moon's soft silvery ray,
    In water to the neck
Lifeless but beautiful he lay—
    A melancholy wreck.

The minstrel from the water-butt
    Himself did extricate;
When what should meet his optic but
    His darling's pa irate,
Who lamm'd him with a cudgel thick
    In fashion most unkind,
The while the faithful dog did stick
    Unto his pants behind.

A warning take, ye youths who read
    This touching little lay,
Perchance 'twill stand you in good stead
    If you should go to pay
Your tribute to some lady fair
    In amatory strain,
Of water-butts, sticks, dogs beware,
    And spare yourselves much pain.

SPRING.

THE zephyrs softly murmur spring
    To tepid airs, and everything
Assumes an aspect fair and gay ;
The skies are deck'd in rich array
Of azure blue and silver grey ;
Exulting Nature seems to say :
" Cold winter's rule hath pass'd away ;
No longer 'neath his iron sway,
In deathly gloom we languish—
Pass'd is our time of anguish."
The angry hyperborean blasts
That fiercely rag'd o'er lonely wastes,
And in green dell and sylvan glade
Such havoc mercilessly made,
Have sought again their native north,
And comes the smiling season forth,
Like captive loosen'd from his chain ;
Now sports fair Pleasure on the plain,
Attended by her jocund train.
The sun diffuses his bright sheen
O'er all th' emancipated scene ;
He scatters with his fiery breath
The darksome mists, the earth, beneath
His ardent, all-transforming glance,
Awakes from her protracted trance,
And yielding snows in livid tide,
Along their sinuous courses glide ;
The husbandman, with ready hand,
Breaks up the loosening fallow land,
And trustfully implants his seed
    In the reciprocating soil,
Then patiently awaits the meed
    Of profit due to honest spoil.
The budding trees in promise show
Summer's ripe charms in embryo ;
The fields with eagerness disown
Their ragged robe of dingy brown
For a sweet garb of tender green ;
Enraptured with the lovely scene,
The little birds begin to mate,

And loud of coming pleasures prate.
The clamorous rook, with noisy zest,
On swaying bough constructs his nest ;
Hear we the cuckoo's plaintive note—
Sweet harbinger from sphere remote—
And blithely through the meadows gay
The sportive lambkins frisk and play ;
Now gambolling with awkward stride,
Anon, crouching at their mothers' side.
See we the pretty flowers again
Bespangling o'er the verdant plain—
Fair daffodils, the violet blue,
Pale buttercups, primroses too ;
The crocus pure and snowdrop white,
The crimson-crested daisy bright,
The wallflower sweet in mingling brown and yellow,
And pretty stock with fragrance richly mellow ;
Rich foretastes of the scented dowers
That lavish Flora on us showers.
Welcome ! thrice welcome ! gentle Spring !
Bearing to us on lightsome wing,
Like beauteous bird of omen good,
Array'd in all thy plentitude
Of charms, thy tide of joy and mirth
To cheer our long-expectant earth.
Dear Spring ! the aged look for thee
With sober-eyed expectancy,
While Memory back to them doth bring
Bright visions of their life's sweet spring,
When all the prospect seemed most fair,
And all unknown were grief and care.
Young folks, with more impulsive gaze,
Wait eagerly thy sunny days ;
Pale invalids, with longing eyes,
Look for thy sunny, genial skies,
So they may quit their sad sick room,
With all its loneliness and gloom,
To breathe thy balmy vernal air
And gaze upon thy beauties fair.
True type of sunny-visaged Hope,
Whose aid enables us to cope

With all the varying ills of life ;
And in the midst of all its strife,
Her radiating beam displays,
And bids us look for brighter days ;
Welcome in all thy pleasing arts,
Thou gladdener of human hearts ;
With blandishment and witching wile,
With pearly tear and sunny smile,
Rule us awhile with kindly sway ;
All, all thy opening charms display,
And onward point our sanguine gaze
To Summer's grand imperial blaze.

BRADFORD V. HALIFAX.

THE Bradford came down like a wolf on the fold,
But for once in a way were awfully sold ;
Poor little Joe Haweridge was very soon done,
And Ritchie ne'er fram'd once to get in a run.

Alas! for poor Bonson, their pet and their pride ;
How galling to see all the tactics he tried
Foil'd time after time by Schofield and Buck,
Who, tho' lacking in size, are Goliaths in pluck.

And their forwards, too, fairly were run off their feet
By their clever opponents, so dashing and fleet ;
Amongst whom Cope, Wilkinson, Dennis, and Clowes
Made one of their best and most brilliant of shows.

Suffice it to say that the close of the game
Saw a fresh triumph added to Halifax fame,
And Bradford once more clearly prov'd they're unable
To turn upon Dodd's merry players the table.

There was general rejoicing all over the town
That the almighty Bradford again had gone down ;
For the Halifax folk never happier seem
Than when their pets vanquish the "Gentlemen's Team."

Whatever on earth will Bradfordians say
This dreadful disaster to argue away ?
They can't find a loophole, but this, don't you see—
They were minus their umpire—the fam'd *"A.B.P."
        *A. B. Perkins.

LIFE'S ALCHEMY.

AS olives crush'd 'neath heavy weight
    Emit a perfume rare,
Which, wafted on the gentle breeze,
    With fragrance fills the air;
So many a precious thing of earth
To pain and sorrow owes its birth.

Oft from some troubl'd bosom, crush'd
    Beneath a load of care,
The fragrant odours are diffus'd
    Of virtues rich and rare;
Virtues, whose lustre shines more bright
Than glittering silvery stars at night.

Oft 'tis some trying circumstance
    In Life's mysterious plan
Whose pressure tends but to enhance
    The real worth of the man;
Yes, often Suffering's crucial test
Evokes all that is truest, best.

When everything is going right
    'Tis easy to be strong,
But manhood's grit is best display'd
    If, when affairs go wrong,
Men face them with undaunted heart,
And play the truly manly part.

Oft Sorrow's subtle alchemy
    Wise Nature doth employ
To separate effectually
    The gold from the alloy—
And mean, ignoble, base desires
Are killed by Pain's consuming fires.

In Music's complex scheme we see
    That Joy's resounding strain
Oft meets and blends harmoniously
    With minor chords of Pain;
So when sweet notes and discords meet
Life's harmony becomes complete.

ONLY A CIRCUS CLOWN.

ONLY a simple circus clown,
   Careless if Fortune smile or frown,
I dance, I sing, I joke and tumble,
My repertoire a perfect jumble ;
A medley strange, kaleidoscopic,
Embracing every varying topic.
With pride my motley garb I wear ;
My watchword is " Begone, Dull Care ! "
To please mankind 's my happy mission ;
I am society's physician,
Administering pleasant pills
To cure the social body's ills.
I open wide the radiant portals
Of Mirth's gay hall to weary mortals ;
'Tis mine to make them laugh and smile,
Their cares and troubles to beguile.
Still, though I aim to make folk laugh,
I sometimes mingle with my chaff
Wisdom and Truth's immortal grain ;
I scatter o'er Life's dreary plain
Stray gleams of Wit's refulgent light ;
I in my humble way unite
The humorous and philosophic ;
And though a section misanthropic—
The captious, hypercritic folks—
Fall foul upon my little jokes,
And dub them " fossils," " antiquated,"
" Chestnuts " rehabilated,
Yet others, easier to please,
Receive my funniosities
And at my cranks and sallies roar
As if they'd ne'er been heard before.
As slyly round the ring I peep,
Or over clumsily I leap,
Then tumble in an awkward heap,
My well-known " Here we are again "
Evokes loud laughter's cheery strain.
E'er fresh to them 's my oldest quip,
And when I seize the Master's whip
To make the pony jump at will,

ONLY A CIRCUS CLOWN.

Their shrieks the bright arena fill.
Ah, thoughtless souls, they see in me
But merriment and gaiety,
While oft is rankling in my heart
Sad Sorrow's venom-pointed dart.
They scarcely think a motley vest
Can hide a sorrow-stricken breast;
That he who entertains them so
Can claim acquaintanceship with woe.

* * *

Well do I mind one winter night;
The "House" was full, my heart was light;
As I was entering the ring
Someone the direful word did bring
That my dear wife at home lay dead;
The message well-nigh turned my head;
To leave the place how I did yearn,
But no one else could take my turn.
With whirling brain and phrenzied eye
I clear'd the ring; my usual cry
Rang bravely—"Here we are again."
O, who shall tell the poignant pain
That rung my breast as round I strode,
Watching the lady as she rode!
As she jump'd through the paper'd hoops
I strove to utter joyous whoops;
I did my tricks, my sayings gay
I struggl'd manfully to say;
But, no, my nature would have vent,
And, to the great astonishment
Of all assembled in the place,
The tears cours'd down my painted face,
As the poor clown, with anguish wild,
Wept in the circus like a child.

* * *

Long weary years have passed away
Since that e'er memorable day;
I've trod the path of life alone
And many cares and trials known.
I strive to overcome my grief,
And find sweet moments of relief

In trying to enliven others.
Methinks this life of ours, my brothers,
Is something like a circus ground,
Wherein we wander round and round,
In tawdry tinsel bravely dress'd;
Where bitter sigh and sparkling jest,
Sweet songs of pleasure, dirges drear,
Rich rays of hope, dark clouds of fear
Mysteriously meet and blend.
And thus my way I onward wend,
A pupil in gay Humour's school,
A simple-hearted roving fool;
No better thing of Fate I ask
Than strength for each day's varying task,
And mirth's irradiating ray
To cheer the darkness of my way.
And when my circus days are done,
This life's mysterious journey run,
It may be He Who reigns above,
The God of Goodness, Grace, and Love,
Will on me leniently look down,
Though only a poor circus clown.

AN INVOCATION TO NATURE.

SWEET Nature, o'er me breathe thy magic breath,
And wake my spirit from its sleep of death;
Encircle me with thy irradiant wings,
And from this sordid scene of mundane things
Transport me far to some congenial clime,
Unmarr'd by discords, passions, follies, crime.
To thy hid beauties ope my heavy eyes,
Command my dormant powers to arise,
Before me wide unfold thy noble plan,
Display the destiny of finite man.
Arise, my soul, and spread thy fleeting wings,
And let us leave awhile these worldly things—
This scene of mingling meetings and farewells,
Gay wedding peals and sad funereal knells;
Where puny man fumes out his little day,
To Fate's caprices but the helpless prey;
This cunning game wherein the craftiest win,

Where might is right, and poverty a sin.
Here spotless Virtue clad in tattered rags,
With aching feet limps o'er the cruel flags,
While Gorgon Vice with arrogant display
In Fortune's car glides tranquilly away;
Fat Opulence glares at the sons of need,
Regarding them as of inferior breed.
Birth, rank, and wealth—the social trinity,
The modern Baal, the sovereign deity
To whom mankind inflect the servile knee;
Where man's apprais'd not by inherent worth
Or genius, but accident of birth.
Ah, nobler he who proudly stands erect
In all the dignity of self-respect—
The grandest sight in all this earthly plan,
An honourable, upright, manly man—
A scion true of Virtue's noble race,
With goodness, truth imprinted on his face;
Upon whom Honour from her shining throne
Hath set her seal and claimed him as her own;
In naked majesty of worth array'd
Scorning to learn the sycophant's vile trade.
How mean is he, tho' clad in courtier garb,
By meanness thriving, while the pointed barb
Of outrag'd conscience wounds his guilty breast,
Filling his soul with discord and unrest!
But Nature's son, enraptur'd with her charms,
Shunneth alike the wide inviting arms
Of syren Pleasure with her fleeting joys,
And proud Ambition's dearly purchas'd toys.
Dearer to him the peaceful rural scenes,
Where Nature reigns, most beauteous of Queens;
Where lovely objects everywhere abound,
Brought by the changing seasons in their round.
Enlist me, Dame, within the faithful band
Whose joy it is to serve at thy command;
I fain would swell the ranks of that brigade,
True followers of the sweet Æonian Maid;
Her tuneful songs I fain would learn to sing,
And soar aloft on Fancy's eagle wing
Until I reach the beautiful retreat,
Parnassus high—the Muses' native seat.

WHO IS MY NEIGHBOUR?

WHO is my neighbour? Is it he
 Whose house adjoins my own,
 Whose lot in life is thrown
Within the same community?

Is he my neighbour, who repairs
 With me to the same shrine;
 Whose voice ascends with mine
In alternating psalms and prayers?

Who is my neighbour? He whose creed
 Is quite in harmony
 With tenets held by me,
And greets me with a warm God-speed?

Is he my neighbour who at will
 With ease displays
 The glorious rays
Of knowledge, scientific skill?

My neighbour is that hapless soul—
 That child of want
 With hunger gaunt,
O'er whom Misfortune's billows roll.

My neighbour is that man of crime
 On Ruin's brink,
 From whom we shrink,
His manhood blighted in its prime.

My neighbour is that thoughtless youth;
 My duty is
 In kindliness
To speak to him in soft reproof.

My neighbour is that peevish child
 Who weakly moans;
 Its fretful tones
Be mine to soothe with treatment mild.

The Indian with swarthy skin,
 The African,
 Or Yellow man,
Are all my neighbours, kith and kin.

My neighbours everywhere are found—
　Where'er I roam,
　Abroad, at home—
Scatter'd to Earth's remotest bound.

SPEAK NO ILL.

SPEAK no ill of one another
　Brethren, as ye tread Life's way—
Remember each man is your brother,
　Say the best that you can say.

Children of one common Father,
　Dwellers in one common clay,
'Stead of harshness should the rather
　Mutual tenderness display.

Speak no ill, but fondly cherish
　Charity within thy breast—
Let all spleen and rancour perish,
　Overcome by that kind guest.

Speak no ill, no, not when even
　You are call'd to suffer wrong;
Forgive, if you would be forgiven,
　Bear it patiently; be strong!

Speak no evil of your neighbour,
　Be not false or insincere;
Be not doubled-tongued, but labour
　To preserve a conscience clear.

Judge not harshly when some error
　Lies beneath your righteous gaze;
Be pitiful, fierce censure's terror
　Ne'er won sinners from their ways.

Speak no ill, but striving rather
　To do all the good we can,
We shall please our Heavenly Father,
　While we bless our fellow-man.

"ACTIN' WEBB."
(A Briggus "do.")

FROM Halifax one summer day
    Some hardy youngsters bent their way
To spend a jolly afternoon
Down at Brookfoot. Behold them soon
Where Calder pours along in pride
His silvery pellucid tide.
From where they stand they hear the brawl
And rushing of the waterfall.
'Twas natural that such a scene
Should bring before their fancy keen
Niagra fam'd and poor Webb's fate;
Whose doughty deeds to emulate
One daring youth the thought conceiv'd.
He in his inmost heart believ'd
That safely o'er the aforesaid falls
His frame could float; so of his smalls
He very soon himself divested,
And sportively the current breasted.
With pride he takes his varying strokes—
Now "breast," now "side"; their little jokes
His comrades crack at his expense,
While he enjoys himself "immense."
Then one got in below the fall,
In order if he heard him call
For help, to render all the aid
He could. "But he was not afraid," he said;
He'd heard chaps say to do it "reight"—
To keep the body firm and straight
Was all a fellow had to do,
And let the current pull him through.
So quite convinc'd that he was right,
The youth prepar'd him for his flight.
At first he got on very well,
But "lack-a-day," sad truth to tell,
His head shot under, and his feet
Were overturn'd, and a complete
Grand series of somersaults
And unexpected graceful vaults
He turn'd. With ooze and slime as black as ink,

The refuse wash'd up from the " Stink,"
His frame was cover'd, and his bones,
Through contact with the cruel stones,
Fair "wark'd" again. O what a plight
The youth was in, and what a sight
Did he present as to the shore
He struggl'd!   How his mates did roar
With laughter at his sorry figure ;
He was as black as any " nigger !"
But sympathising with his griefs,
They clean'd him with their handkerchiefs ;
He left the spot in sober truth
A sadder and a wiser youth,
And as he homeward took his way
He to his trusty chums did say :
" I won't act Captain Webb no more ;
I have had sufficient I am sure."

CHARITY.

("And now abideth Faith, Hope, Charity, these three, but the greatest of these is Charity."—Corinthians xiii., 13.)

I SING the praise of Charity,
   That precious priceless rarity,
     O would that we could see,
Amid the darksome noxious weeds
Of unkind words and loveless deeds,
     More of its radiancy.

What pregnant seeds of grief and woe
Do man's inhuman actions sow
     Within the soil of life,
That duly in the social field
Bring their inevitable yield
     Of malice, discord, strife !

How chang'd 'twould be, if only man
Would study Nature's kindly plan,
     And, in its workings, see
How seeming hostile forces move
Each in its own appointed grove,
     Yet blend harmoniously.

CHARITY.

Yon golden sun that gilds the plain,
Soft dews and fertilizing rain,
   The frost, the changing wind—
Divergent paths they all pursue,
With one grand, common end in view—
   The good of human kind.

And shall these senseless forces roll
Concordantly to their great goal,
   And godlike, reasoning man,
By envy, malice, rancorous ire,
By thoughtless selfishness conspire
   To mar the noble plan?

Ah no! within the heart's deep cell
Rich chords of music latent dwell
   Which, waken'd from above
By Charity's resistless hand,
Shall rise and fall in cadence grand,
   The harmony of love.

In what doth Charity consist?
In heading a subscription list?
   In giving to the poor?
Altho' 'tis noble work indeed
To minister to mortal need,
   Still it does something more.

In comprehensive, kind embrace
It fain would fold the human race,
   And know nor castes nor creeds;
Asking no party shibboleth,
And having but one rule of faith—
   Not empty words—but deeds.

True Charity with tender art,
Seeks to relieve the wounded heart,
   To comfort the forlorn;
Doth e'er with sympathetic voice
Rejoice with those who do rejoice,
   And mourn with them that mourn.

It doth not vaunt itself on high ;
Nor view with supercilious eye,
   As of inferior breed—
Those rear'd in Poverty's rude shed,
'Mid dire privation nurtured,
   The hapless sons of need.

Doth not with exultation scan
The errors of a fellow-man,
   But with a kindly voice
Bids a poor wand'rer try again
Virtue's fair pathway to regain,
   While angel hosts rejoice.

If to these ends our varying powers
Were spent, Love, Joy, like lovely flowers,
   Would sweetly spring to birth ;
All Discord's jarring notes would cease,
And Plenty, universal Peace,
   Prevail upon the earth.

Thus let us pass Life's fleeting days,
In varying spheres and varying ways
   Contributing our share
To usher in Love's golden reign,
That our dark earth may bloom again,
   Like Eden's garden fair.

For Faith and Hope must fade away,
Ending with Life's little day,
   But greatest of the three—
Triumphant o'er the conquering tomb,
Immortal Charity shall bloom
   Through all Eternity.

THE YOUNG.

THE sanguine spirit of the young
   In roseate-tinted sheen
     Gilds every opening scene

Of Life ; Hope with her flattering tongue
Singeth to them inspiring measures ;
  Fancy waves her magic wand
  And opens out her pictures grand—
A realm replete with sweetest treasures
  Springs up before their eager gaze ;
  They bask them in the golden rays
Of youth's irradiant, vigorous sun ;
  Onward impell'd by keen Desire,
  On steps that never seem to tire
Athrough the busy course they run ;
They roam through Pleasure's golden palace,
  Nectar draughts of joy they quaff
From her brimming sparkling chalice ;
  With beaming eyes and merry laugh,
    Launched upon Life's swelling tide,
    Lightsomely their vessels glide ;
    Nought reck they of reefs and shoals,
    Careless, hopeful, sanguine souls.
Pale-fac'd Care with wrinkl'd brow
  From the scene averts his gaze ;
  He quits the uncongenial clime,
  And sullenly abides his time,
Which cometh soon he well doth know ;
  Future dark untoward days,
When he shall sheathe his rankling dart
Relentlessly in each sad heart.
  Ah ! youthful spirits, have your day,
  Be ye happy while ye may !
  Dream your bright illusive dreams,
  Treasure up the beauteous gleams,
  Revel in your fairy bowers,
  Pluck the rainbow-tinted flowers,
  Fill with bliss each fleeting day,
  All too soon will come the fray,
  With its tumults and alarms,
  Angry skies and clashing arms,
  When Fancy will have had her day,
  And stern fac'd Fact will wield the sway ;
  Then youthful souls, be blithe and gay,
  December soon doth follow May.

THE PORTRAIT OF A CRITIC.

I'M a self-appointed mentor, and it is my little plan
    To try and make myself as disagreeable as I can ;
cultivate assiduously a pleasant little way
Of being most offensive in what I have to say ;
My highest happiness it is to wound the human heart,
Give me the tiniest loophole, and with consummate art
The keen edge of my sarcasm will I insinuate ;
In all the varying games of life I strive to demonstrate
O'er all mankind my measureless superiority ;
So if you'd see a genius just turn your eyes on me.

My little mission is to feed the flickering flame of art,
To science, music, poetry finality impart ;
A lengthy start can I concede to Mr. Oscar Wilde,
And all the Nine regard me as their dearest fav'rite child.
If he were here I would not fear illustrious Apollo,
While as for Socrates and Co., I'd simply beat them hollow.
In the glorious realm of rhetoric I could with greatest ease
Eclipse the classic Cicero, or great Demosthenes ;
In short, search all this planet, and find me if you can
Just such another talented and versatile a man.

With "eye-glass in my ocular" and classic brow severe,
The bosoms of beginners do I inspire with fear ;
I make a great impression upon inexperienced youth,
Who regard me as an oracle, the fountain-head of truth ;
No kind of game do I regard as *infra dignitatem*,
Youth, age, or beauty, all alike, relentlessly I slate 'em ;
"Week in week out, from morn till night," away at them I hammer,
At this one's weak chronology, another's shaky grammar ;
Full many a literary brow of laurels have I shorn,
And made the wretched scribblers wish they never had been born.

Behold me in my sanctum as o'er the newest serial
I flash my eagle optic with glances magisterial,
I sentence pass upon it in something like this style—
The orthography is dreadful, the syntax simply vile.
I ne'er in all my lifetime read such execrable "rot,"
The writer has no notion of working out a plot ;
The people are insipid, the thoughts are bald and crude,
And never quit the region of threadbare platitude.
The manuscript I then dismiss without another look,
And bid the author burn it and try to write a book.

Perchance a wretched dabbler in mediocre verse
Invites my kind attention while his lines he doth rehearse
I note his trepidation, although he strive to mask it,
And cheerfully I mention the editorial basket ;
I note his look dejected as I smiling hint that he
Must not expect to mount far up the great Parnassian tree,
Then for his delectation I crack a little joke
About the flame poetic but ending oft in smoke ;
And as away from me he turns with disappointed sigh,
"There ! I think that's settled him," exultingly say I.

Should a man send me a letter that is somewhat poor in style,
A rich vein of amusement it affords me for a while ;
I show the wretched missive to acquaintances in town,
And it is music in my ears to hear them run it down ;
I care not for the poor man's want of opportunities,
To ridicule his errors doth my fancy richly please ;
What's that I hear you murmur—a breach of etiquette ?
That is one of the few things I have to learn as yet,—
That such a genius as I must be kept down by rules
Formulated for the guidance of prim old-fashion'd fools.

But 'tis when at the opera I'm seen in all my glory,
I take in with a single look the principals before me ;
My ample stock of lyric lore I air with look profound,
And raise my voice so it may reach the people sitting round :
The contralto and the tenor they cannot sing at all,
While as for the soprano—Lord, how the jade does squall !
And the deep portentous frown that gathers o'er my face
Displays my disapproval of the efforts of the bass ;
They're but a set of marionettes, I say contemptuously,
It ne'er was my misfortune a poorer lot to see.

And if I'm ask'd the question by some carping critic elf,
How it is I never think of doing anything myself ?
My answer is, why can't you see, I really am so throng
Discovering the many ways where other folk go wrong,
Besides—this little fact you have to bear in mind—
My forte is the destructive, not the constructive kind ;
And thus it is I pass the even tenour of my days,
Content with showing others the error of their ways ;
My occupation, like Othello's, is gone if my wit
May not display by noting other people's want of it.

A QUIET MIND.

THERE is a precious priceless gem;
   No brilliant in a diadem
Can boast a ray so pure, refin'd,
That gem of gems—a quiet mind.

Some seek for bliss in Beauty's glance,
Or Pleasure's giddy mazy dance;
More lasting bliss is theirs who find
The heartsease of a quiet mind.

The dwellingplace where fancies sweet,
Calm thoughts, and feelings exquisite
In loving union are combined,
Is that sweet cell—a quiet mind.

Though circumstances conflict wage,
Though trouble's tempest swell and rage;
We can meet all with heart resign'd
If we possess a quiet mind.

The friends in whom we would confide
May prove as changeful as the tide;
No friend more constant can we find
On earth, than this—a quiet mind.

Why mourn if the decree of Fate
Assign to us a lowly state—
Her hardest blows, howe'er unkind,
Are harmless to a quiet mind.

Rank, riches, honour, power, name,
Ambition's guerdon—deathless fame,
What are they?—baubles all combin'd,
Compar'd unto a quiet mind.

The splendid son of lofty birth,
With all the good things of the earth,
Is poorer than the poorest hind,
If he have not a quiet mind.

With heart prepar'd for good or ill,
Endurance, courage, strength of will,
Victor o'er all earth's ills combin'd
Is he who hath a quiet mind.

CONSIDER THE FLOWERS.

CONSIDER ye the flowers
    That brightly deck the field ;
Mark well the many lessons
    These voiceless teachers yield ;
How powerfully they witness
    Of His unceasing care
Whose Providence arrays them
    In garniture so fair !

Consider ye the flowers,
    In grace and beauty dight,
Studding Earth's velvet carpet,
    Creation's jewels bright ;
The lily's spotless whiteness,
    The daisy's ruddy hue,
The yellow-tinted primrose,
    And violet darkly blue.

That King of mighty wisdom—
    Judea's royal sage—
Who fathom'd all the knowledge
    And learning of his age ;
In all his regal splendour.
    His wealth from distant seas,
Was not—the Scriptures tell us—
    Array'd like one of these.

If God so clothe the flowers,
    That bloom so fair to-day,
Which fade and droop to-morrow,
    And then are cast away ;
Much more His human children
    Shall clothèd be and fed
By Him, Whose Love hath number'd
    The hairs upon their head.

TRIP TO THE ISLE OF MAN.

(The incidents herein recorded really took place, the parties being all Halifax people, who supplied the Author with the materials for the following effort.)

IN dismal weather cold and grey,
One Monday morn there sail'd away
From Blackpool's pier a noble craft—
The celebrated " Bickerstaffe."

Upon the deck a group of ten—
Six maidens fair, and four young men,
With merry faces, spirits high,
A close observer might descry.

About the deck they sport and run,
As they anticipate the fun
That waits them at the Isle of Man—
Towards which fast as e'er she can

The vessel hastes. O sad to tell
The misadventures that befell
These maidens six, and young men four,
Ere they were landed on the shore !

That dreaded scourge, alas ! is there,
Which French folk title *mal de mer.*
That terror of the rolling main
Siezed first of all upon Miss Jane.

It very quickly laid her low,
And downstairs soon she had to go,
Where, stretched upon the cabin floor,
She firmly vow'd that never more

Would she attempt to cross the main
Aboard the " Bickerstaffe " again,
Which pitch'd so awfully that day
As *hors de combat* thus she lay.

In another corner of this barque
A young man of the name of Park
Outstretch'd upon his beam-ends lies,
Viewing with sympathetic eyes

A lady in the pain's fierce grasp,
Supported by the timely clasp
Of a tar who volunteered to go
And see her safely down below.

Another youth with prudent heed,
In his sad time of pain and need
Clung to a spar, nor loos'd his hold
Lest overboard he might be roll'd.

Close by him were an aged couple
Loudly lamenting o'er their trouble;
O take me home, my Nannie, cries
The old chap as he rolls his eyes.

Another youth then feels the qualm,
And calls out to his comrade Sam:
O deary me, I feel so queer;
Fetch me a drink of nettle beer!

And one called Tom, as low he lies,
Unto his tender sweetheart cries:
O Annie, kindly let me rest
My weary head upon your breast.

And there the lot of them lay spuing,
The sailors their nice task pursuing
Of waltzing round with mop and bucket,
To catch it in as up they chuck it.

Two sisters of the name of Reed
Were very very bad indeed;
So very bad in fact were they,
That on the deck they could not stay.

But how to get them down below
Was something none of them did know,
Till Steward took them 'neath his care,
And help'd along the luckless pair.

At length, suffice it for to say,
They reach'd their journey's end that day;
And awful mad were they to find
The boat at least four hours behind

The stated time, as on the shore
They quite expected to have four
Clear hours at least the Isle to view ;
Instead of which there's nought to do

But for each weary sea-sick sinner
To try and pick a bit of dinner,
And then to plough the briny main
Aboard the " Bickerstaffe " again.

We won't attempt their weary track
To follow as they journey back.
'Tis said 'twas nine o'clock and past
When they reach'd Blackpool's pier at last.

Each of them more than satisfied
With what the " outing " had supplied ;
Resolv'd Old Neptune to explore
On board the " Bickerstaffe " no more.

THE PARTING.

THE sad dark hour draws on apace,
   My dearest love, when we must part,
To wander for a dreary space
   In different scenes ; but in our heart
Will we erect a temple fair,
   In it each other's form enshrine,
And e'er in thought to it repair,
   Our hopes and thoughts to intertwine
In true Love's firm indissoluble bond,
And thus to grow more constant and more fond.

Farewell, my darling love, farewell !
   Alas ! I cannot longer stay ;
Hark, hear you not the cruel bell
   Imperious calling me away ?
But when o'er distant seas I roam
   My fond thoughts aye will fly to thee,
As darts my vessel through the foam
   Oft like a vision shall I see
Through storm and dark thy lovely face
In spirit fold thee in my fond embrace.

AN AGED PILGRIM.

(In memory of the Author's Grandmother.)

A N aged pilgrim worn with years,
    Bow'd down beneath the load of Time,
Hath left this realm of sighs and tears—
        This mortal clime.

Encompass'd in her earthy bed,
    Commingling with her kindred clay,
Now rests she with the tranquil dead
        From Life's stern fray.

With patient constant faith she bore
    Her cross along Life's thorny road,
Her eyes fix'd on that radiant shore—
        The saints' abode.

Athrough the gloomy vale she pass'd,
    And laid Life's heavy burden down—
Her long'd-for haven gained at last—
        Her golden crown.

O'er her no more shall tempests sweep,
    Nor harsh winds of adversity;
No earthly ills can break the deep
        Tranquility.

Death came to her as welcome friend,
    He came to bid her sorrows cease,
And guide her with a gentle hand
        To endless peace.

She holds the victor's fadeless palm,
    Her feet now tread the golden street,
Now joins she in the ceaseless psalm—
        Heaven's anthem sweet.

With those who long long years ago
    By Death were torn from her embrace
She meets, no parting e'er to know—
        Meets face to face.

WAIFS AND STRAYS.

Waifs and strays—what tongue can tell
    The woes that in those three words dwell?
There lies within the sentence brief
A very universe of grief.

Waifs and strays—poor hapless ones,
Earth's suffering neglected sons;
Cold is the heart that cannot bleed
With sorrow for their bitter need!

Waifs and strays—who sadly roam
Without a friend, without a home;
Their footsteps follow'd by the gaunt
Grim apparition, grinding Want.

Waifs and strays—o'er whose dark way
Hope never throws a golden ray;
To them appears no prospect bright,
But all is dark as densest night.

Waifs and strays—no kind caress,
No mother's smile to cheer and bless;
No father's teachings sage and kind
To fortify, instruct the mind.

Waifs and strays—no lofty aim
Their feeble stunted powers claim—
Their highest hopes, their greatest good,
But perishing material food.

Waifs and strays—O boasted land
Of light and truth, uplift thy hand—
In tenderness and Christlike love
This stigma from thy midst remove!

Waifs and strays—philanthropists,
Be yours to dissipate the mists
That cloud the path of needy youth;
Implant the seeds of virtue, truth.

Waifs and strays—O ye who know
No pang of want, no bitter woe—
List! list! unto the piercing cry
Of these poor souls who round you lie!

Waifs and strays—up, Chistian world !
Let Love's bright banner be unfurl'd ;
Inaugurate a new crusade
'Gainst Evil's hostile hosts array'd.

Dear Albion, arise in might,
And take thy stand for truth and right ;
Unite all parties, creeds, and classes—
Thy watchword grand, Reform the Masses !

MORN.

THE blushing morn hath risen
    From his orient bed,
Back to their gloomy prison
    Nightly shades are fled.

Brightly Aurora beams on
    The wak'ning scene beneath her,
With blending purple and crimson
    Staining the fields of ether ;

Uprising vapours wreathing
    The mountain's rugged brow ;
Delicious odours breathing,
    The breezes softly blow.

The pretty flowers awaking
    From Slumber's close embrace,
Bright pearly dewdrops shaking
    From their forms of grace.

Birds with enchanting measure
    Hail the happy hour,
O'er all the prospect Pleasure
    Reigns in gentle power.

The grand High Priest of Nature—
    Yon majestic sun—
The beauteous portraiture
    Beams benignly on.

Man, awake from slumber,
    View the gorgeous sight ;
Add your tuneful number,
    Praise the morning light !

EXPERIENCE.

EXPERIENCE is a pedagogue
   Of aspect cold severe—
He has a large academy—
   He rules his school by fear;
His scholars are the human race,
   The world at large his sphere,
And for the lessons he imparts
   His charges oft are dear.

He teaches by the specious tongues
   That spoke us seeming fair,
And then our confidence abus'd—
   Entrapp'd us in a snare;
'Tis often by his painful aid
   Betwixt the false, the true,
We learn how to discriminate
   Which to retain, eschew.

And oft some pupils fail to learn
   The lessons he would teach,
Regarding not the useful lore
   He puts within their reach;
But blindly grope along engulph'd
   In darksome gloom of night,
As if they had no eyes to see
   His guiding beacon light.

Oft, warn'd by him, we learn to shun
   The bright alluring snare;
When wavering 'twixt right and wrong,
   In solemn tones " Beware!"
He cries—" rash mortal, stay thy foot,
   Shame, bitterest remorse
Lie in the pathway; turn about
   And choose a wiser course!"

His teachings are as medicine
   That, bitter to the tongue,
Like tonics on the feeble frame
   Do act and make it strong;
That knowledge we most dearly prize
   For which we have to pay,
And oft it is through Sorrow's night
   We pass to Joy's fair day.

Some quickly take his lessons in
  While others are but slow ;
On such, their wit to accelerate,
  He deals the frequent blow.
And some there are so dull that e'en
  He needs must fail to teach—
Reason and judgment strive in vain
  Their darken'd soul to reach.

He shews to us the wisest plans
  By which results are gain'd ;
How Life's unnumber'd purposes
  Are easiest attain'd ;
In every varying path of life,
  In Labour's field or mart,
Embracing Science's domains,
  The beauteous realm of Art.

He daily to each one of us
  In tones of warning cries ;
Would we his premonitions heed
  We were the truly wise.
Then let us heed his guiding voice,
  And spare ourselves the pain
And ills that surely follow them
  To whom he speaks in vain.

TO A ROSE.

PURE fragrant thing, whose lovely hue
  And tender form present so true
  A type of mortal state ;
In thy frail beauty we may trace
Resemblance to our fragile race,
  And emblem of our fate.

Thy destiny—to bask awhile
Beneath the bright sun's genial smile,
  Array'd in brilliant bloom ;
To flourish for a transient day,
And then to languish and decay,
  O'erwhelmed in deathly gloom.

FADED LEAVES.

POOR faded leaves, my spirit grieves
    To see you lifeless lying,
Or whirling round with rustling sound,
    Before the rude wind flying.

Yellow and sere, while darkness drear
    Enshrouds the face of Nature;
Dun leaden skies hide from our eyes
    Her beautiful portraiture.

O'er hill and dell the fun'ral knell
    Of Summer's sadly ringing,
In eager bands to distant lands
    The birds their flight are winging.

When gentle Spring his rainbow wing
    Wav'd gaily o'er the prospect,
How fresh and green your forms were seen,
    How fair then was your aspect!

When Summer fair cast everywhere
    Rich gleams of golden glory,
And skies were dight in sweet warm light,
    And Hope told her bright story,

I saw ye then in wood and glen
    Amidst the flowerets pretty;
The birds would come to your calm home,
    And sing their love's sweet ditty.

Now Autumn brown looks sadly down,
    His eyes the teardrops laving,
The shivering trees in the chill breeze
    Their thinning branches waving.

Pale yellow leaves, my spirit grieves
    Thus to behold you lying,
In your sad fate the fragile state
    Of man exemplifying.

THE SPIRIT OF SPRING.

THE spirit of Spring
    Is a-murmuring
This genial April day ;
    All seems to wear
    The promise fair
Of merry smiling May.

    Old Winter keen
    With deep chagrin
Perceives his empire ended,
    And in dismay
    He hies away
By his cold blasts attended.

    The primrose yellow
    And his fair fellow,
The lily of the valley,
    Like stars of light,
    Shine gaily bright
In many a vernal alley.

    The skies a veil
    Of silver pale
Wear o'er their mantle blue ;
    The drifting crowds
    Of fleecy clouds
Are ting'd with many a hue.

    Flora, coy maiden,
    Comes richly laden
With sweetest earliest treasures,
    The soft south breeze
    Amid the trees
Murmurs its soothing measures.

    All Nature's voice
    Calls out " Rejoice ! "
O heart of man, be gay ;
    With pleasure greet
    This season sweet,
And cast your care away

THE RETURN TO WISDOM.

RESPONSIVE to thy gentle voice,
   O Wisdom fair, my errant steps,
That from thy pleasant paths so long
Have stray'd, again to thee I bend,
From dazzling Folly's winding maze.
And all those transitory things
That o'er my feeble will so long
Have rul'd with iron despotic sway.
I come again to thee, and yield
My lowly homage, and that love
So long withheld, but now restor'd.
Too long have I thy lovely charms
And tender winning wiles withstood.
All vainly thy inviting voice
Hath sounded on my heavy ears,
Summoning me unto thy side;
My blinded eyes refus'd to see
Thee beckoning with thy gentle hand,
And pointing up the rugged steep
Of Duty. But I turn'd from it
To follow Inclination's bent,
And yielded up to worldly joys
My powers, in th' eager search
Of phantom Pleasure, all bewitch'd
By her voluptuous form and voice
Of syren sweetness, whose loud notes
Quite overwhelm'd thy gentler tones.
Enslaving my enraptur'd heart,
She led me captive at her will,
And soon o'er me attain'd complete
Ascendancy, and all the love
That formerly for thee I felt
Seem'd vanquish'd by this new-found love.
Beneath her bright seductive smile
(So like the wreckers' deadly fire
Shining athwart the stormy sea
To lure the vessel to her doom)
I long did bask, and fondly hugg'd
The chains that did my soul enthrall.
Long time in this " Fool's Paradise "

Did I sojourn, until at length
Her draughts of nectar 'gan to pall
Upon my taste, her luscious fruits
To ashes turn'd upon my tongue,
The halo, which around her head
Imagination's hand had thrown,
Vanish'd, and one by one her charms
Seem'd leaving her each time I gaz'd;
Until, of all her tinsel stript
At length, and in the balance true
Of Reason weigh'd—the crucial test—
Calm Judgment then, in sternest tones,
Pronounced her wanting in those things
That minister to highest need,
And lacking the sweet healing balm
To mitigate the pains that Time
Inflicts, possessing not the power
To nourish in man's craving soul
Those aspirations lofty, great,
That e'er should find a dwelling there;
And destitute that subtle skill
Wherewith to heal a wounded heart,
All impotent the soul to cheer
In that most gloomy trying time,
When treasures fail, and friends depart
And leave the bosom vacant, sad,
Like some deserted banquet hall,
When all the revelry and mirth,
Delicious music, dancers fair,
The garlands gay, resplendent lights,
Have faded from the lonesome scene.
Or in the hour when all our hopes,
Like flowers fragrantless and dead,
Lie scatter'd o'er Life's dreary plain
Before the wind of adverse Fa e—
Those flimsy structures that our minds
Have elevated with such care,
Demolish'd by the ruthless hand
Of hoary Time, the fell destroyer!
'Twas thus Reflection, with a train
Of haunting memories, sojourn'd

Within the cloisters of my mind :
Before the haze-dispelling rays
Of light from Truth's translucent sun,
The mists and clouds that so obscur'd
My mental vision were dispers'd,
And then I saw with wond'ring eye
The labyrinthine devious paths
Through which my inconsiderate steps
Had rashly swept, in quest of that
Fleet frolic Pleasure, that so oft
Appear'd within my eager grasp,
Then vanish'd like the false mirage,
Which to the traveller's wistful eye
Presents o'er arid desert wastes
The semblance of an oasis,
The thought of whose refreshing shades,
Reviving waters, feathery palms,
With hope upbuoys the sinking heart,
And to the nigh exhausted steps
Of man and beast afford new strength
To strain to reach the welcome spot,
And then in disappointment dire
And dark despair enshroudeth all
By fleeing from their longing eyes
Just when relief appears most near !
Then how Regret's deep mournful tones
Swept through my agitated breast
When I perceiv'd my idol lie
Shatter'd and wreck'd, upon whose shrine
I all my varying gifts had laid,
My manhood wasted, strength abus'd,
And talents, opportunities,
All irrecoverably lost,
Flung recklessly by me away !
The miserable fatuity
I deeply cursed that led me on
The hollow shadow to pursue.
Then. as to Jewry's Sage of yore,
Life's total sum appear'd to me
But all as emptiness itself ;
The baubles I so highly priz'd

And fondly to my bosom clasp'd
Seem'd now with adder's venom'd tooth
My very vitals' strings to gnaw;
Like ghastly spectres to my sight,
That mock'd and jeer'd me in my pain.
And then methought the substance real,
Of life in all its power and grace
To me appeared, in glorious garb
Of truth, and virtue, spotless white;
It shew'd to me that happiness
In earthly good doth not consist;
That mere enjoyment cannot yield
Unto the never-dying soul
The highest good, the truest gain.
I likewise saw that peace and joy,
In all their fulness are but found
In ever hark'ning to the voice
Of Duty, and her high behests
To conscientiously fulfil;
To toil with zeal unquenchable
To benefit and bless our kind,
And labour bravely to remove,
To our abilities' extent,
Some of the evils that afflict
And scourge our poor humanity.
To wage a fierce incessant war
'Gainst everything ignoble, mean,
And ceaseless seek to manifest
In countless ways our interest
In everything whose object is
The welfare, progress of Mankind.
To cheer the weary drooping heart,
Sinking beneath the storms of life,
By deeds of love and kindliness;
To seek in tenderness to win
Some erring spirit to the side
Of virtue, honour, self-respect;
To strive to tear the darkening veil
Of ignorance from off the mind,
And let the radiant beams of truth
Shine into every dark recess;

To censure justly when some deed
Of wrong, of grasping fraud arouse
Stern Indignation's furnace glow,
To let kind Pity's precious tears
Flow freely forth when in the ear
Is breath'd the mournful tale of woe—
The recital of pinching need;
To deal forth with unstinting hand,
As stewards of a gracious Lord,
The bounties of our scrip and store,
And alleviate the pangs of want.
This is to live, and truly live,
In sweet accordance with the plan
Of Him Whose gracious will it is
That all the creatures of His hand
Should, in the intercourse of life,
By tender love reciprocal,
And mutual dependency,
In tolerant forbearance due,
And world-embracing charity,
Diffuse around reflections bright
Of His own glorious attributes.
This is the soil in which the soul
May flourish, and a harvest rich
Of bliss ineffable e'er reap.
Each little ministry of love,
Or noble act of self-denial,
Each effort on behalf of Truth,
And every prayer to Heav'n breath'd
O'er some benighted wanderer,
Or lonely vigil nightly kept
By bedside of the helpless sick,
The wise reproof in love addressed
Unto the ear of reckless youth,
Are enter'd in that volume great,
The Book of Life, where names of saints
Are ineffaceably inscrib'd
By the recording Angel's pen.
This our imperishable renown,
The glorious unfading prize
To summon forth our noblest powers—

Eternal life in yon blest realm--
Where ceaseless antiphons of praise
Are render'd by enraptur'd hosts,
Souls everlastingly redeem'd ;
Safe in their haven long desir'd,
From mundane tribulation free ;
There, where no surging waves of sin
Disturb the deep tranquility ;
Pain, fear, and anxious doubt no more
Depressing influences exert ;
No ill can reach those happy souls,
Emancipated from the chain
Of finite frail humanity,
Basking beneath the dazzling light
Proceeding and deriv'd from Him,
The Lamb, Who is the Light thereof.
This then, my soul, thy lofty aim—
To tread the pathway of the just,
To dedicate thy time, thy gifts
Unto His glory, Whose thou art ;
That thus the priceless hours of life,
Which, once gone, ne'er can be recall'd,
May find thee, as they wing their flight,
Wiser, and nobler, and more true ;
Reflecting ever in thy path
Rich rays of the transcendent light
Of Him Who lighteth all the world.

THE HERO.

ACCORDING to the vulgar mind,
True heroism would we find,
Grim Battle's gory fatal field
Doth highest type of heroes yield.

They tell us that the "man of war"
A hero is superior far
To those who in a peaceful sphere
Their country serve from year to year.

They picture him amid the glare
Of lurid flames, when trumpets blare,
And cannon bright and bay'net keen
Engag'd in mortal strife are seen.

THE HERO.

But are no heroes to be found
Save only on the tented ground?
Does sanguinary Mars supply
The highest form of chivalry?

Ah no! heroes as true as great
Are found in varying estate,
Amongst the sons of lowly name,
As well as those of rank and fame.

He truly is a hero, who,
At Duty's summon's ever true,
Discharges well his daily task
And honestly disdains to bask

In sunshine of the great man's smile
By dint of simulating guile,
And play with double-minded cant
The rôle of servile sycophant;

But clad in Virtue's white array
Will tread Life's journey day by day;
His watchword, Honour, Truth his guide,
And take his part with manly pride.

A faithful husband, parent dear,
A trusty comrade, prompt to cheer
With ready aid and sympathy
At sound of Sorrow's plaintive cry.

With kindly comprehensive mind
He suffers with his suff'ring kind;
No stickler he for forms and creeds,
His rule of faith, not words, but deeds.

He e'er with patriotic pride
Rallys around his country's side,
Foremost in Danger's gloomy hour
To stand against a hostile power.

This man, whatever his estate,
A hero is, true, noble, great;
However lowly his degree,
Or ill preserv'd his pedigree.

THE GREEN DELL.

I LOVE the lone dell in its fair robe of green,
   When the bonnie blue harebell and violet are seen,
As the sweet breath of summer perfumes the soft breeze,
While winds murmur soft in the foliag'd trees;
When songsters' sweet notes on the balmy air swell,
Yes a beauteous place is the lonely green dell.

How fair is the view when Morn rosy bright
Bathes mountain and vale in its orient light,
The sombre dun clouds scudding swiftly away,
Unable to cope with Aurora's bright ray;
O would I could picture the beauties that dwell
In the prospect when Morning smiles on the green dell!

How gorgeous the aspect reveal'd to the gaze
Contemplated when Noon's meridian rays
With a mantle of gold enfold the fair scene
And heighten the tint of its vesture of green;
Then the heart of the lover of Nature doth swell
As he feasts on the charms of the lonely green dell.

Sweet is the green dell in its soberer mien,
When Evening presides o'er the fairy-like scene;
Old Sol's grander glories have faded from sight,
Reluctantly yielding his rule unto Night;
And Solitude throws over all a deep spell,
I love then to roam through the lonely green dell.

When the wearied out birds droop their head on their breast.
And tranquilly in their green coverts rest,
The flowerets drooping their beautiful heads
While the silvery dew glistens bright on their beds,
And plaintive night breezes their soft moanings swell
How soothing to roam through the lonely green dell!

CRICKET MATCH—"GUARDIAN" v. "COURIER."

(With apologies to W. S. Gilbert.)

I HAVE a song to sing O
   What is your song O
'Tis the doleful theme of a cricket team,
   Who played to a laughing throng O
To the Fountain Head, with bosoms gay,
They went their foemen proud to play;
They did their best, but lost the day,
And sad at heart they came away—
   Beat by the men of the *Courier.*
     Heyde, heyde,
     Misere me, lackaday-de;
   Their pains are o'er,
   They'll play no more,
     All through meeting the *Courier.*

I have a song to sing O
Sing us your song O
'Tis a mournful strain of woe and pain,
   For the *Guardian* team went wrong O
The George-street lads were like to fall
When their two best bats came out first ball;
It flayed 'em so they could hardly crawl
   To the sticks to face the *Courier.*
     Heyde, heyde, &c., &c.

I have a song to sing O
This is the song O
The winners' glee o'er their victory,
   But they must not crow too strong O
Nor lift their noses high in air;
For some who saw the game declare,
Had the *Guardian* "Fielding" been all there,
There wouldn't have been a deal to spare
   In the scoring of the *Courier.*
     Heyde, heyde,
     Misere me, lackaday-de,
   The match is o'er,
   So *Au revoir*
     Says the *Guardian* to the *Courier.*

NIGHT THOUGHTS.

I LOVE the peaceful hour when night
  In garb of sombre sable dight,
Fix'd firmly on her ebon throne,
Enfolds the scene from zone to zone,
And o'er a weary slumb'ring world
The ensign of her power unfurl'd
Serenely floats o'er land and sea,
When grassy mound and verdant lea,
Copse and woodland, vale and hill,
Are wrapp'd in silence deep and still ;
Earth's thousand noises lull'd to rest
Upon her round revolving breast.
As when in robe of tender blue
The boundless sky appears to view,
Upon whose ample bosom clear
Numberless myriads appear
Of tiny stars, their taper light
Twinkling tremulously bright,
With sparkling scintillating gleam,
Like gems in regal crown they seem.
Or when the pale queen of the night
Sheds o'er the earth her mellow light,
Enveloping the mundane scene
In a bright vest of soften'd sheen ;
Her mellow all-pervading beams
Appear like lucid silvery streams
That softly gild the sloping hill,
Reflected in the waters still.
Illuminating winding glen,
Tangl'd brake, and mossy fen,
Lingering with fond desire
On the tapering village spire ;
Or tranquil wood's sequester'd ground,
Breezes wandering around
Where the birds and flow'rets rest,
By the calm God oppress'd
'Tis then, O calm mysterious Night,
I love to ponder with delight
Upon thy charms. At such an hour,
I own thy soul-subduing power.

Then, then, my feeble lyre would raise
Her humble notes of grateful praise
In tribute to each pleasing charm
Of thy fair beauty chaste and calm.
But not thy beauties, Night, alone
Call forth the eulogistic tone ;
Other attributes thou hast
Of worth and virtue unsurpass'd.
As when the wearied sons of men
Have laid them down to woo again
A respite brief from toils and care,
Thy busy gentle hand repairs
The ravages that labour, thought,
Upon their feeble frame have wrought,
And, yielding to thy soft embrace,
They enter on a transient space
Of balmy undisturb'd repose,
And each thy freshening power knows,
Equipping him again to play
His part in the approaching day,
When in the world's arena great,
Each in his varying estate,
Performeth his respective part
In lonely field or busy mart.
Not only for thy healing power,
O Night, love I thy stilly hour:
Thou hast for me peculiar charms
E'en in the tempest's wild alarms ;
As when the wind from feeble moan
Increases fast in strength of tone,
Until in culminating roar
Of mighty strength it rages o'er
The prospect, dashing o'er the plain
In proud contempt and high disdain.
All, all are phases dear to me ;
In all my fancy seems to see
Such secret views of Nature's power
As well repay the frequent hour
I've spent in reverie and thought,
Profound excogitations fraught
With aspirations deep and strong

Unto the poet's varying song.
How pleasant, too, the musing hour,
When, 'neath the spell of Mem'ry's power,
Our fond thoughts travel swiftly back
Athwart the dim expansive track
That Time's fleet footstep intervenes
Between the past and present scenes;
As through the vista of past years
We fondly gaze, how bright appears
The light of days forgotten long;
What varying emotions throng
As old associations dear
Before us rise distinctly clear!
With eyes bedimm'd with tears we see
Familiar scenes, where blithesomely
In childhood's sunny hour we stray'd,
The flowery dell, the winding glade,
Where Nature rob'd in all her charms
Bath'd the pure air in fragrant balms.
O sweetest hours of purest joy,
  Untainted by Sin's foul alloy!
How oft our roving restless eye
Gazed up to the great wide sky,
Viewing with childish innocence
The wonders of Omnipotence!
Oh, with what tender subtle sky
Those precious hours of childhood still
Their blissful memories interweave
Amid the warp of things that grieve.
When mourning o'er Temptation's power,
We pass the lonely midnight hour,
Then 'tis that o'er the troubl'd breast
A wave of yearning unexpress'd
Sweeps o'er the ocean of our pain.
We would that we were young again.
When sinful thoughts and deeds of shame
Imperious the attention claim,
And Memory's relentless hand,
Imprints, as with an iron brand
A sense of Sin's tyrannic power,
And self-condemn'd we sink and cower.

Then, then, we bitterly contrast
The present with the blissful past,
And sigh and yearn, but all in vain,
For Childhood's innocence again.
O ye who from fair Virtue's way
May tempted be to err and stray,
When Sin's allurements seeming fair
Present the subtle specious snare,
And Passion's fierce devouring fire
Prompts the lascivious desire ;
Raise, raise the earnest prayer on high,
That He Who rear'd the vaulted sky,
Whose all-controlling power doth sweep
Resistless o'er the mighty deep ;
Form'd the round world and all therein,
Will 'twixt the surging waves of sin
And your frail natures interpose,
And scatter wide your deadly foes.
If thus from guile ye guarded be,
And every thought of evil flee,
Ye ne'er shall dread the nightly hour,
Nor Mem'ry's reproducing power ;
Then shall your path through Life's rough way
Be lighted by Hope's guiding ray ;
Each day some sweet new link supply
Connecting you with days gone by,
Until Life's fleeting race is run,
And Immortality's begun
In yonder blessed realm of light,
The home of bliss, where there's no night.

A TRIBUTE.

(Lines written on picking up a small volume of poetry, written by a poor working man, whose name the Author cannot remember.)

MODEST little volume,
   Clad in lowly guise,
Plain and unattractive
   Unto vulgar eyes ;
Homely basket holding
   Fruit and flowers fair ;
Casket plain enfolding
   Jewels rich and rare.

Studded thy small pages
    With rich gems of thought,
Meet for learned sages,
    From experience brought;
Fruit of pleasant flavour,
    Nurtur'd in the soil
Of honest brave endeavour
    Mid Life's weary moil.

Bread upon the waters,
    By thy Author cast,
In unlikely quarters
    Found maybe at last
By some kindly spirit,
    After many days,
So that patient merit
    Wins its meed of praise.

THE POET'S WORLD.

THE poet inhabits a world of his own,
    A realm of his own creation;
His mind is his kingdom, his fancy his throne,
    His wealth his imagination.
His fleet-wingèd thoughts are the slaves of his will,
    Aye ready to go where he sends them—
To roam over lake, meadow, valley, and hill,
    Wherever his pleasure commands them.
True lover of Nature in every phase,
    His eye can perceive her fair beauty,
Conceal'd from the worldling's material gaze;
    Her service is bliss, not mere duty
Perform'd in a cold, perfunctory way,
    But a deep, ever-deepening pleasure,
The heart's willing yielding to Nature's soft sway;
    Yes, this is the bard's richest treasure.
He knows that the mistress he faithfully serves
    Is as kind as she's peerlessly beauteous,
A handmaid benign whose heart never swerves
    From her followers patient and duteous.

A PASTORAL.

YE Shepherd swains, to me give ear,
   See, bright Sol hides his glowing crest
Behind the curtains of the west!
And mild-eyed Evening draweth near
In dusky robes and shimmering veil.
With visage beautiful, tho' pale,
She walks the ethereal streets along
Attended by a brilliant throng
Of courtiers clad in silvery sheen,
Bright subjects of a beauteous queen.
The wearied birds are slumbering,
Deep stillness wrappeth everything;
The flow'rets close their starry eyes,
And like a pearly necklace lies
The dew upon each slender stem.
Æolus breathes a requiem
O'er the departing gleam of day;
The owlet from the turret grey
Utters its piercing plaintive cries;
Round the blind bat whirling flies.
The lover to the lonely grove
Telleth the story of his love;
He tunes his lowly Doric reed
To her, alas! who will not heed,
Soft Lydian strains, which, as they swell,
Interpret but alas! too well
The pangs that in his bosom dwell.
Ye shepherds, all due watch must keep,
From danger guard your helpless sheep
That in the fold contented feed;
As night approaches, pay due heed
Lest Reynard come, the wily thief,
With gleaming eye and cruel teeth;
Or wolf that bays with hollow cry
The moon as she sails calmly by.
Shepherd swains, to me attend,
Well your helpless charges tend;
If one weary eye must sleep
Let the other vigil keep,
Till the first faint crimson ray
Herald the approach of day.

POVERTY.

OF all the ills that flesh is heir to
   There is not one to be compar'd to
The cursèd ill of poverty;
In it exists, it seems to me,
A multifarious misery,
The aggregate of all the woes
That agitate and discompose
The mighty sea of mortal life,
And wrack the human breast with strife.
Foul source prolific from whence flow
Dark streams which poison as they go.
Frail mortals, render'd desperate
By want, privation, perpetrate
Actions from which their hearts recoil;
But, tempted by the thought of spoil,
They haste to satisfy their needs
By ruthless predatory deeds.
How often, too, the beauteous maid,
In youthful innocence array'd,
Is yielded up a sacrifice
To him who bids the highest price;
Perchance, to save the family pride,
Becomes a sad, unwilling bride—
Warm youth allied to palsied age,
Condemn'd, poor soul, upon Life's stage
To represent her wretched part,
Who gives the hand without the heart.
Or mark that youth whose thoughtful brow
The stamp of genius doth show;
Converse with him, and you shall find
He has superior powers of mind;
His eyes beam with intelligence,
But galling, grinding indigence
Holds him within its iron chain;
His mental labour is in vain:
The world at large may never know
The mighty, glorious thoughts that glow
Within the furnace of his brain;
Hence grand inventions with their train
Of useful offspring may be lost

For lack of means to pay their cost.
See Virtue, bow'd 'neath heavy load,
Limp painfully along Life's road,
Winning but by incessant strife
His daily bread, the prospect rife
With doubt, anxiety, and fear.
As he surveys his lov'd ones dear,
Misgivings well nigh whelm him o'er
Of what the future hath in store.
The invalid with pale, worn face,
Who longing yearns for change of place—
The health-imparting genial air
Of some salubrious climate, where
A rest from Life's unceasing strain
May bring back health and strength again.
Alas! against such luckless mortals
Are firmly clos'd the pleasant portals
Leading unto the happy ground
Where ease, rest, peace, and hope are found.
Yet have I, wondrous to relate,
Heard prolix orators dilate,
With unctuous sonorosity
On the blessedness of poverty;
Employing sundry pious saws
And platitudes about the laws
Of Nature, to persuade their hearers
To see the beauties of such theories.
They strive to shew 'tis Heaven's will
That some should eat and drink their fill
Of Earth's good things all through their life,
While others have its care and strife.
But me these preachers but amuse
As they express their simple views
With prim, smug face, and pious air;
'Tis easy work for those who share
The benefits which means afford—
To say—O trust ye in the Lord!
Commit yourselves unto His care
Who, in His gracious goodness ne'er
Will see His children lacking bread.
I sometimes fancy, if instead

Of favouring us with such discourses,
These worthies from their own resources
Would help the poor, whose pain and care,
They from the pulpit oft declare
They do so earnestly deplore,
They'd do a very great deal more
To win the masses to their side
Than oratory's flowing tide,
However orthodox and true,
Will ever have the power to do.

A JINGLE.

YE men of the rhyming fraternity,
   Upon whom with smiles of maternity
  The Goddess divine
  Doth tenderly shine,
Bright Poesy's gay confraternity.

Ye courtiers in Nature's sweet palaces,
Who quaff from her joy-laden chalices,
  Whose mystical art
  To each poetic heart,
Ambition, joy, comfort, and solace is.

Unlearned in lore academical;
Remote far from factions polemical,
  Philosophical schools
  Where they lay down the rules
Of *leges* mechanical, chemical.

Bred and born in Worth's doughty democracy,
To which the dull-brain'd mediocrity
  Has admittance denied,
  In spite of his pride,
Though a scion of earth's aristocracy.

Though the world at large pay little heed to you,
Materialists say there's no need for you;
  Yet this sad world of ours
  May be cheer'd by the flowers
Ye throw o'er its path, so God speed to you.

WHERE ARE THE NINE?

WHERE are the nine? in accents sad
    Once ask'd the Christ, Who came to men
To heal their souls and make them glad:
    But one return'd; were there not ten?

Where are the nine? there is but one!
    Sadly exclaim'd the Son of Man,
To thank God for the mercy shewn,
    But one—this poor Samaritan.

Long centuries have roll'd their course
    Since Jesus trod Life's weary way;
And yet, with still increasing force,
    The question might be ask'd to-day:

Where are those souls on whom the Lord
    So much of earthly good bestows?
Alas! sad answer to record—
    But one of ten whose bosom glows

With warmth of genuine gratitude.
    Alas! how very few who raise
To Him, the Giver of all Good,
    Tributes of grateful, heartfelt praise.

Shall He Who op'd His sacred veins
    To cleanse us from a fouler blot
Than leprosy's dread, loathsome stains:
    Can such a Saviour be forgot?

Lord! in Thy boundless plenitude
    Of power and grace, our hearts endue
With never-ceasing gratitude,
    And strength to follow Thee anew.

Acknowledging in all our ways,
    Eternal Lord! thy love and power,
O be Thou with us all our days
    Our Hope, our Wisdom, and our Tower!

AN AUTUMN MEMORY.

ONE afternoon in Autumn,
    The sky was drear and gray,
Absorb'd in meditation
    I took my lonely way.

It was in Essex County,
    Near unto Ingatestone—
A little rural hamlet
    Sequester'd and unknown.

Most dreary was the prospect—
    The trees were well-nigh bare;
No birdlings' merry trilling
    Resounded on the air.

The hedges were all dripping
    With freshly-fallen rain;
The breeze was sadly moaning,
    Like one in mortal pain.

As if in sore displeasure,
    The Sun withheld his ray;
In sodden'd yellow clusters
    The dead leaves thickly lay.

Gleam'd through the tangl'd hedges
    The berry's crimson head;
The tiny acorn cower'd
    Within its leafy bed.

No sound disturb'd the stillness
    But the cawing of the crows,
Sitting in solemn conclave
    Upon the leafless boughs.

All Nature was a-mourning,
    Her darling Summer fled,
And freely fell her teardrops
    Upon Earth's humid bed.

And as I stroll'd on, musing,
  The solemn passing bell
'Gan suddenly a-ringing
  Its sad resounding knell.

Then, gazing up the roadway
  Far as the eye could see,
I dimly saw some figures
  Slowly approaching me.

Becoming then quite curious
  To know what this might be,
That seem'd like a procession
  Advancing steadily;

My laggard step I quicken'd
  Into an eager stride,
And in another moment
  A touching scene I eyed:

'Twas a little funeral party
  Walking with solemn tread,
Bearing a tender infant
  Unto its earthy bed.

No sable plumes were nodding
  In sombre gorgeous state;
No pageant incidental
  To obsequies of the great.

There was the tiny coffin
  Borne on a farmer's cart,
Drawn by a little donkey,
  That seem'd to play its part

Just as the human mourners,
  Walking with subdued tread,
A young child held the bridle
  And gently strok'd its head.

The broken-hearted parents
  Follow'd the lowly bier,
Throbbing with deep emotion,
  Shedding affection's tear

O'er the sweet bud they cherish'd,
  Now fragrantless and dead,
The day-star of their dwelling,
  Their light of life now fled.

With thoughts too deep for language
  Gaz'd I upon the scene,
The lowly little cortège,
  The parents' sorrow keen,

Until a pathway leading
  Unto the burial place
The little party enter'd,
  And faded from my gaze.

THE GIFT OF POETRY.

AS wandering breezes careless sweep
    The strings of an Æolian lyre,
Awakening Music from her sleep;
    So often the poetic fire
In richest waves of fervour rolls
O'er many unknown lowly souls.

Just as from each unconscious string,
    Sway'd by the breeze's gentle power,
Rich varying chords of music wing
    Their flight athrough the stilly hour—
So oft from lowliest sons of earth
Come tender strains which owe their birth

To some mysterious power within,
    Beneath whose hidden gentle sway,
They calmly move amid the din
    And conflict of Life's fleeting day—
A beautiful refining guest,
The joy, the solace of their breast.

A treasure to the world unknown
    Oft by some nameless one possessed;
How rich the spirit that doth own
    A gem so rare, his lot how bless'd!
To what grand heights may he not rise
With such a rich and precious prize!

THE PRIEST'S SECRET.

(Suggested by a picture in Gray's window.)

'TIS now the tranquil placid hour
   Of Evening, bird, beast, and flower
Are wrapp'd in undisturb'd repose;
Day's wearied monarch downward goes,
Illuming with his dying gleam
Hill, landscape, meadow, winding stream.
Pale Cynthia, Creation's queen,
Benignly vieweth the fair scene—
On high she hangs her silvery lamp;
The faithful stars with steady tramp
Patrol the wide ethereal camp.
In friendliness they seem to smile
Upon the gray cathedral pile—
Scintillating, trembling, gleaming,
Through the colour'd windows streaming,
Blending with the sacred light
On the altar burning bright,
Softening the cold grey stone;
While the Vesper's solemn tone
Floating on the stilly air
Calls the monks and nuns to prayer.
Pass they on in holy column,
While rich music grandly solemn
Through the massy fane is roll'd
From the organ's mouth of gold;
As, in the antique chamber high,
Absorb'd in fervent rapture, I
Touch with a sympathetic hand
   The polished keys, and melting chords
Summon forth at my command—
   Strains too beautiful for words,
Which, as they vibrate and roll
Flood with bliss my listening soul.
Then Fancy, from her hid retreat
Comes forth outspreading pictures sweet,
And Memory rings her dulcet bells,
Binding my soul with magic spells—
Presenting to my wistful gaze
Familiar scenes of bygone days:

My village home I fondly view,
  Live o'er again my happy childhood;
  Again I roam the tangl'd wild wood,
Follow the stream that meander'd through
Its mossy banks with rippling sound;
The busy windmill whirling round,
Whose noise the village seem'd to fill;
The ivied church upon the hill;
The breezy, pleasant, ample green,
Of artless mirth the frequent scene:
That tree with spreading foliage,
With seats beneath, whence wearied age
Could view the pleasures of the young,
Or gossips ply the unwearying tongue.
I see again our dear old cot—
That dear lov'd well-remember'd spot—
In fancy almost seem to catch
The creak of its old rusty latch.
My father sage, my mother dear,
Then to my tearful eye appear—
Long years have pass'd since they were laid
To rest beneath the yew tree's shade.
And O! oft comes a vision fair—
A face of beauty wond'rous rare—
My dear lost love beside me stands,
She seems to spread her snowy hands,
And fix on me her large deep eyes;
  Then, as within my eager grasp,
  Her beauteous mould I strive to clasp,
Away the lovely vision dies,
Leaving my soul engulph'd in gloom
As darksome as the cheerless tomb.
And then the old, old weary pain
With freshen'd force comes back again;
The wound I fancied Time had heal'd
Re-opes, my heart that I had steel'd
Against the blind God's wild delight,
Again acknowledges his might;
For I, the pledg'd and tonsur'd priest,
A secret hold within my breast
Which nought but Death can e'er remove—

The secret of a long-lost love.
Long years ago I lov'd her well,
Her heart it throbb'd reciprocal;
She was my sun, my star, my life,
I sought to win her for my wife;
But merciless parental pride
   Decreed her loftier position;
She must not be a poor man's bride,
   And on the altar of ambition
My beauteous love was offered up.
Ah me! O bitter was the cup—
Two lives their cursed pride did sever;
With tears we parted, and for ever.
I could not bear my simple home,
   I was a hopeless homeless ranger;
Where'er my weary steps did roam
   Gladness unto my heart a stranger.
I wander'd sadly up and down,
Through sleepy hamlet, busy town,
Or ancient cities of renown—
A stranger traversing strange ground—
Until my weary footsteps found
A refuge in the quietude
Of this, a holy brotherhood.
The priesthood's solemn vows I took
And worldly things for aye forsook.
Oft times, as in my lonely cell
In meditation deep I dwell,
Will come to me a blissful thought
With sweetest influences fraught,
That nerves me for my life of trial,
Of penance, vigil, self-denial.
The brethren as they calmly go
Upon their way will never know
The under-current of unrest
That finds a lodging in my breast.
O precious thought! there comes a day
When all Earth's clouds shall melt away,
And I and my lost love will meet
In Eden's beauteous garden sweet.
Nought, nought the perfect bliss shall mar,

In the sweet song no discords jar,
Nor pride parental raise a bar
Our tranquil souls to come between ;
But free from sorrow, free from sin,
Unfetter'd by the fleshly chain
   Of this poor mortality,
We'll roam the fair Elysian plain
   And drink of true felicity.
Roam amid the beauteous bowers
Deck'd with amaranthine flowers,
While enraptur'd myriads string
Their harps to the Eternal King.

    *   *   *

Thus cheer'd along my pilgrim way,
I journey on from day to day ;
Succouring the sick, the poor,
Bringing from the plenteous store
Of my heart's experience sad
Sympathy that maketh glad
Many sorrowing hearts around
Fainting on Life's battle-ground.
Fill'd with holy thought and deed,
Fly the days with swiftest speed,
Bearing me to that sweet clime,
The rest beyond the hill of time.

A VOICE FROM THE SKY.

SEATED by my ingle bright
   On a dreary winter night,
I ponder'd o'er my luckless plight,
     Weary, alone,
While whirl'd the snow in furious flight
     And winds did moan.

I saw my expectations cross'd,
The hopes I so long cherish'd lost,
Like flowers nipp'd by Winter's frost
     And cast away ;
Or vessel water-logg'd and toss'd
     On raging sea.

A VOICE FROM THE SKY.

Methought that I had been mistaken
In the course which I had taken—
All my confidence was shaken—
      Sad was my heart;
I griev'd that I had undertaken
      The minstrel's art.

All silent was my feeble lyre,
No faintest spark of Nature's fire,
Responsive to my fond desire,
      Cheer'd with its ray;
My weary feet and heart did tire
      Of Life's hard way.

A deep despondency fell o'er me,
All darksome was the way before me,
And, like an ocean wildly stormy,
      My bosom heav'd;
With none to cheer, to reassure me,
      I deeply grieved.

Thus brooding my misfortunes o'er,
I rose and strode my cottage floor
Awhile, then open flung the door,
      And on the sky
I gaz'd, as Boreas wild did roar,
      With pensive eye.

In dense black clouds the sky was dight,
Sweeping along in swiftest flight
Before the tempest's gathering might;
      Up gazing far,
I saw amid the gloom of night
      A bright red star.

And then I saw a huge black cloud
Enfold it as within a shroud,
Then pass away, while clear and proud
      The star still beam'd,
Laughing defiantly and loud
      To me it seemed.

'Twas blood-red Mars, and then as I
Stood watching him with eager eye,
Methought that from the distant sky
    The star did call,
Like silver clarion ringing high
    That thrill'd my soul.

He cried aloud, the hero bright :
O mortal, faint not in the fight ;
With patience climb the rugged height,
    Through all your foes
Cutting your way till Fortune's light
    Upon you glows.

Strengthen'd by that heroic star,
Fixed in his blazing battle-car,
Again I armed me for the war,
    That winter night,
Resolv'd that nought my course should bar
    To Fortune's height.

A LIFE THOUGHT

TO labour on with cheerful breast,
    To strive to do our very best,
I take to be the proper plan
To be pursued by finite man.
Not idly dream of fate or luck,
But try what industry and pluck,
With hopefulness and patience, too,
Combin'd, will help a man to do.
Choose e'er the right, the wrong refuse,
Look straight before thee, take short views ;
Drink moderately of Pleasure's cup ;
Wait not for something " to turn up "
(Micawber-like), but bravely toil
To win your guerdon fair of spoil
From busy Industry's vast field.
Fight on ; know no such word as yield
Until Death's overwhelming blow
Descend on thee and lay thee low.

THE FIRST PSALM.

BLEST is the man who doth not walk,
   Nor stand in sinners' ways ;
Nor sitteth where the scornful talk
   With bold derisive gaze.

Who from the statutes of the Lord
   Derives a deep delight,
And ponders o'er the Sacred Word
   By daytime and by night.

He shall be like a fruitful tree
   Well nourish'd by the flow
Of waters, in prosperity
   His leaf shall bud and grow.

But with the ungodly 'tis not so,
   Who tread not Wisdom's way ;
They're like the chaff the wind doth blow
   And scatter far away.

For in the dreadful Judgment Day
   These sinners shall not stand,
But seek to hide themselves away
   From His avenging hand.

For all those who His will obey
   The righteous Lord doth know,
But sinners shall be cast away
   And perish in their woe.

THE NEW YEAR.

BORNE swiftly hence by Time's on-rushing tide,
   Hath sped away another circling year ;
And in the Past's dim ocean deep and wide,
   Its joys, its sorrows, fade and disappear.

On the strange current of a new-born year
   We launch the frail vessel of our life,
Athwart its unknown depths our way to steer,
   With mingling hopes, doubts, fears, conjectures rife.

THE NEW YEAR.

The past year with its follies, failures, sin,
　　Vows unredeem'd we never may recall;
To strive to mend our ways may we begin,
　　And to the Heavenly Power for succour call.

Perchance the year just ended may have brought
　　To very many much of care and woe;
Dark troublous times, with deep affliction fraught,
　　Dear lov'd ones by relentless Death laid low.

To such, may be, as if to make amends,
　　This New Year comes with brightly smiling face;
As Heaven its sweetest consolations sends,
　　And sunny smiles grief's bitter tears replace.

We know not what the future hath in store,
　　'Tis from our gaze by love and wisdom hid;
Could we but see what waits us on before,
　　Our hearts perhaps would sink o'erwhelm'd with dread.

Though health, friends fail us, earthly joys be few,
　　And troubles come in like a swelling tide;
There's One that 'midst it all will e'er be true,
　　Who closer than a brother will abide.

If but the Eternal Pilot guide our bark
　　'Twill weather the most trying storms of fate;
It must be well when all appears most dark,
　　Though tempests rage around infuriate.

Let Faith and Hope perform their lofty part,
　　Enabling us to meet the ills of Time
With tranquil mind and with undaunted heart,
　　As those who seek a far serener clime.

This I conceive to be our wisest plan,
　　To labour on, to strive our very best
To raise ourselves, do all the good we can,
　　And leave to All-wise Providence the rest.

With loftier objects, hearts more kind and true,
　　Adorning well our varying estate,
Pursue we then with hope and courage new
　　The untrodden path of 1888.

BURLESQUE V. THE DRAMA.

IT was a beauteous stilly summer night;
   The azure sky was bath'd in lambent light:
Pale Cynthia had hung her silvery lamp
High in the midst of the ethereal camp;
The shining stars—a myriad glittering globes—
Sparkl'd and flash'd like gems on regal robes;
All nature seem'd to rest from labour's throes,
And everything invited to repose.
Ye genii who rule the realms of air,
Ye sportive elves, the reason strange declare
That caus'd the pensive bard to leave his bed
And wander through the chilly streets instead;
As carelessly he murmur'd the refrain
Of some old song, he wander'd down Green Lane;
All heedless as to where his footsteps strayed,
Crossing St. James's Road, down North Parade
Awhile he strode, and then inclin'd his feet
In the direction of Commercial Street;
Thence passing, he his steps did onward wend
Until at length he found he'd reach'd Wards End,
Then near the statue of the Consort good
He paus'd awhile in meditative mood.
     *   *   *   *
As if to rouse him from his reverie,
The Town Hall clock announc'd the hour of three,
And instantly the Parish Church clock too
Asserted that the statement was quite true.
Turning to leave, the Royal met his eyes,
And lo! a sight that filled him with surprise.
A brilliant dazzling radiance seem'd to shine
O'er the dilapidated Thespian shrine,
And, gazing up towards the balcony,
Two lovely female forms the bard did see.
One was a stately tall majestic maid,
In modest robe of sombre hues array'd;
A crown of classic bays adorn'd her head;
She mov'd along with calm and queenly tread.
In sooth she was a noble regal dame,
Of lineage great; the Drama was her name.
The other was a phantom frolic wight,

In flimsy gown of tawdry tinsel dight ;
A merry maiden, gay and picturesque ;
Jolly, bizarre, and rightly hight Burlesque.
She heeded not the other's withering glance,
But with a roguish grin eyed her askance ;
A moment at each other thus they gaze,
And then they spoke in controversial phrase :

DRAMA.

Avaunt, thou giddy elf, and quit my sight !
Poor empty thing in shameless costume dight ;
How darest thou intrude upon the stage,
Sphere dedicate to wisdom deep and sage ?
Burlesque, extravaganza, comedy,
Whate'er thy name, it matters not to me.
Hence ! hence, I say, seek the congenial sphere
Of music-hall, to puerile palate dear ;
And ne'er again intrude upon my sight
In my domains, my home, my place by right.

BURLESQUE.

What means this outburst of bombastic rage ?
Ancient anachronism, who says the stage
By a prescriptive right belongs to thee ?
Old party, you've to reckon now with me.
I care not for your scorn, your haughty mien,
Your angry aspect of an outrag'd queen ;
I quail not at your posings statuesque ;
This fact know thou, that I, despis'd Burlesque,
Have come, and what is more, have come to stay,
In spite of all you choose to do or say.

DRAMA.

Ye sacred Muses ! must I then thus hear
This rowdy ribald glibly at me jeer ?
O public taste, and hast thou reach'd this pass,
To seek thy entertainers from this class—
Mere mountebanks, a giddy careless throng,
The votaries of the dance and comic song ?
The stage should hold aloft to Nature's view
Her likeness touch'd with Truth's unfading hue ;
Paint Villainy, with intricate device,

And reprobate proud, Gorgon-visag'd Vice.
The stage should be an ever-sacred shrine
Erected for the worship of the Nine ;
Here should we learn to shed the pitying tear
With poor Ophelia and mad King Lear ;
View swart Othello's blindly-jealous rage,
Which Desdemona's death could but assuage ;
List moody Hamlet's sad soliloquy,
And learn with noble Brutus how to die.

Burlesque.

Cease, pedant, cease your rhodomontade strain !
Believe me it is utterly in vain.
Mark what I say : the British public shrink
From any play that calls on them to think ;
At home they have enough of that to do
Without it at their entertainments too.
What care they for your Desdemona's woes,
Your Romeo and Juliet's dying throes ?
Who wants to sit and squeeze out maudlin tears
O'er Hamlets, or East Lynnes, or mad King Lears ?
All they desire is just to simply sit
While sylph-like forms before them lightly flit ;
Bask in the sunny beams of Beauty's glance,
And gaze on Pleasure's giddy mazy dance ;
The while the merry pun and catchy song
Conspire to chase the lagging hours along ;
Given half-clad girls, a coster, and a dog,
And nought on earth their happiness can clog.

Drama.

O dire descent from Genius's high planes !
What folly thus to worship limbs, not brains.
Incredible ! It surely cannot be
That people long will rest contentedly
With such unsatisfying pabulum ;
I still will hope the day must surely come
When nobler tastes shall enter on their reign,
And sweep away this empty-headed train ;
In Lethe's Stygian waters them submerge,
From which they never shall again emerge.

BURLESQUE.

Now there you are, old lady, wrong again ;
Your lofty aspirations are in vain.
Make up your mind, you'll never see that day :
Our managers know well it will not pay
For higher things to try and form a taste ;
Their money and their time they will not waste.
Grand Opera even looks on me with dread,
And, bullrush-like, bows a diminished head ;
For, heedless of her wealth of melody,
The public flock to feast their eyes on me.
I take more money in a single show
Than you in all the week, and that you know :
Take my advice, forego your haughty pride,
And promptly range your talents on my side.

DRAMA.

And this to me ! Consort with such as you !
A stupid, vulgar, rowdy, motley crew !
What ! prostitute the genius of the stage,
And pander to a foolish frivolous age ?
What ! win vile gold by fostering low taste ?
No, rather in the desert let me waste ;
Before I'd aid in such a base intent,
To die outright I'd rather be content—

Thus spake the maid in fierce indignant strain,
When down there came a heavy shower of rain,
And in a pensive mood each went her way,
Resolv'd to have it out some other day.

A WORD OF CONSOLATION.

I STOOD within a churchyard
  One sunny sabbath day,
And gazed with sadden'd eyes on
  The tokens of decay
That in such sad profusion
  Bestrew'd the hallow'd ground,
While o'er the peaceful prospect
  A silence reign'd profound.

A WORD OF CONSOLATION.

The stillness was but broken
   By murmurs of the breeze,
Breathing its soft requiem
   Athrough the leafy trees—
A dirge it seem'd to fancy
   O'er those in Death's embrace,
Wrapp'd in tranquil slumber
   'Neath the earth's green face.

Methought, as I stood gazing,
   Each sad memorial stone
With eloquence seem'd gifted,
   And in a gentle tone
Bade me not mourn as hopeless
   Dear ones to rest thus laid,
But think of them as living,
   In fadeless bloom array'd.

And as the melting tear-drops
   Bedimm'd my mourning eye,
And from my bosom's depths came
   A deep, a troubl'd sigh,
Within my ear seem'd sounding
   A sweet, a gracious voice,
In utterances so precious
   As made my heart rejoice.

"Weep not," said it, "I am the
   Resurrection and the Life;
Weep not, for they are blessèd,
   They rest from earthly strife;
Why thus in hopeless sorrow,
   Poor mortal, dost thou grieve?
For they do live for ever
   Who in my Name believe."

Bless'd word of consolation!
   How tranquilly to rest
Sank 'neath its soothing power
   The storm that swept my breast;
And as I left the churchyard
   It seem'd as if a ray
Of brightest heavenly sunshine
   Had fallen on my way.

THE WINTER MONTHS OF NINETY-FIVE.

WITH salt tears streaming down her nose,
    The Muse give utt'rance to her woes,
As I narrate in mournful rhyme
The terrors of an awful time—
A page of history destin'd
To linger long within the mind
Of all among us who survive—
The winter months of Ninety-five.

'Twas on the New Year's natal day
The fell fiend first began his sway ;
With frost and snow, with snow and frost
Alternately to rule the roast ;
With his keen breath, like pointed barb,
That pierc'd e'en through the stoutest garb,
'Twas no light task to keep alive
In those cold months of Ninety-five.

Poor little ones were lacking bread,
And clam'ring loudly to be fed ;
Distracted parents full of care,
Right on the verge of dark Despair ;
Homes destitute of food and fire
Because the toilers wanted hire—
Bees frozen out of Labour's hive
In those dark months of Ninety-five.

Wake, Gratitude, awake the strain !
Tell how the piercing cry of pain
Fell on Benevolence's ears,
And call'd forth Pity's melting tears ;
How Charity, most beauteous dame,
Upon the scene with promptness came.
Sources of succour to contrive
In those sad months of Ninety-five.

All honour to the noble band,
All honour to each ready hand
Uprais'd to scatter wide relief,
And stem the torrent-tide of grief ;
And when is pass'd the time of need,
Oft Mem'ry shall applaud the deed,
How our Borough kept her poor alive
    In those cold months of Ninety-five.

LIFE.

I mus'd in deep perplexity
   On Life's unravell'd mystery,
In all its deep complexity.

I thought on Nature's mighty plan,
And in its working seem'd to scan
A likeness to the state of man.

I on huge mountains cast my eyes,
Saw their colossal summits rise
Until they seem'd to prop the skies.

And nestling lowly at their feet,
The vales array'd in verdure sweet,
Symbol methought most clear and meet,

Of Mankind's varying estate—
Patricians powerful and great;
And plebeians born to lowly fate.

Then I beheld the trackless sea,
Now rapt in deep tranquillity,
Anon upheaving restlessly—

Its alternating calm and strife
A picture of this mortal life,
With mingling joy and sorrow rife.

The heaven with ever-changing scene,
Now deck'd in robes of brilliant sheen,
With clouds and darkness oft between.

And so 'tis with Life's chequer'd sky;
At times all bright, no dark clouds nigh,
Or when no blue can we descry.

The floods that sweep the mountain's side;
Huge rivers rolling in their pride,
And mirthful rills that murmuring glide,

Contributing from varying source,
Each in its own appointed course,
To swell the deep's stupendous force.

So on the breast of Life's strong tide,
Resistless, swelling, deep, and wide,
The human currents onward glide
Till verberates from shore to shore
Great Gabriel's dread trumpet roar,
Proclaiming Time to be no more.

TO SCOTLAND.

HAIL, " Bonnie Scotland," beauteous land !
   I sing thy prospects bright and grand—
Heav'n-touching azure-mantl'd mountains,
Thy silvery streams and dancing fountains,
Unrivall'd panoramic views
Deck'd in innumerable hues,
Turgid torrents fiercely sweeping,
Silvery cascades lightly leaping,
Romance's favourite retreat,
Sweet Poesy's own native seat.
Mother of Bruce, of Burns, of Scott,
Can such a country be forgot ?
Where Nature picturesque and rude
Reigns in her wildest grandest mood.
Vast moors extending to the view
Huge seas of mingling brown and blue,
The sombre heath and waving dell,
Home of the pretty heatherbell,
Pure Patriotism's fairest shrine,
Flooded with Freedom's light divine ;
Thy fiery-hearted sons have broke
For ever the oppressor's yoke,
And freely pour'd their life's rich tide
To keep intact thy ancient pride.
The theatre sublimely grand
Hast thou been, O illustrious land,
Of many a great momentous drama
In Time's swift rushing panorama.
Would that I had a Burns's lyre
Swept with the true Æonic fire,
That I might fitting pæons raise
O glorious country, to thy praise !

THE POET'S JOY.

I ENVY not the rich, the great,
   Their golden store, their grand estate,
Their splendour and their luxury,
Or long ancestral pedigree.
I see the children of ambition
In eager quest of power, position,
A famous name, a place at court,
And not a single envious thought
E'er finds a lodging in my breast,
Though oft by earthly ills distress'd.
Though Fortune's darlings pass me by,
Or bend on me a scornful eye,
I have within me stores of wealth
Which all their hoards of golden pelf,
However great, can never buy—
A gift bestow'd by Heav'n on high.
This is my all, my better part,
The Muse's secret mystic art.
Ah, yes, though poor and feeble be
The strains the Goddess giveth me,
They yield to me a vein of joy,
And find my powers sweet employ.
She is the star that cheers my lot
And brightens up the tiny spot
Where my unhonour'd lot is cast;
My refuge from the howling blast
Of fickle Fortune's adverse wind;
The peace that solaces my mind
When Poverty and carking Care
Would leave me prey to dark Despair.
When Grief's sharp pangs assail my heart,
When trials come, and friends depart,
Then in the constant Muse I find
A healing balm, a friend most kind.
Though rude and halting be the strains
I raise, although to reach the lofty plains
Of Helicon's harmonious height,
Where burns the grand Æonian light,
I fail, and may not emulate
The songs of bards of lofty fate,

Those gifted souls whose names sublime
Adorn the lustrous scroll of Time,
Still, humbly following in their wake,
My lower path through Life I'll take,
Contented with a few stray beams
From Poetry's translucent streams;
My one great hope, my chief desire,
The real, the true poetic fire.

A NIGHT REVERIE.

OLD Sol hath run his race diurnal,
   And yielded unto shades nocturnal,
In silence wrapt the hills eternal
      And slumbering streams,
Fair Cynthia with smile maternal
      Upon us beams.

The trembling stars their vigils keeping,
Bright meteors o'er empyrean leaping,
Soft dews in glistening silver steeping
      The pretty flowers,
With curl'd-up petals, calmly sleeping
      In fairy bowers.

The restless zephyr softly blows
Wand'ring 'mid the leafy boughs,
The glowworm's lantern brightly glows,
      With deep delight,
The darkness-loving owl forth goes
      To greet the night.

Far out upon the mighty deep,
While wearied sailors soundly sleep,
The watch his lonely guard doth keep
      With cheery ray,
The little stars down on them peep,
      And guide the way.

By Slumber's weighty breath oppress'd,
The labourer takes his well-earn'd rest,
No cares disturb his honest breast,
      No terrors move,
Peace brooding o'er his humble nest
      Like gentle dove!

The wily poacher spreads the coils,
Anon he views the feather'd spoils
Entangl'd in his cunning toils,
    Safe in the snare,
And triumphs inly as he foils
    The keeper's care.

Alas! O Night, beneath thy shade,
In Sin's fair panoply array'd,
To ply the harlot's hellish trade
    Doth shameless go
That frail one erst a guileless maid,
    Now fallen low.

The sentinel with steady tramp
Paces around the tented camp,
Mid pestilential vapours damp
    And beasts of prey,
Till Morning lights his cheery lamp,
    And 'gin's the day.

Oft o'er and o'er again do I
Athrough the solemn hour lie,
While busy Fancy forth doth fly
    From her retreat,
And spreadeth out before the eye
    Her pictures sweet.

What care I for the loss of sleep,
A rich reward of bliss I reap—
Inspiring thoughts and lessons deep
    My toils requite,
And my poetic senses steep
    With deep delight;

Oft as thy solemn hour comes round,
O peaceful Night, shall I be found
Ready to roam the ethereal ground
    Of fancy bright;
My love for thee still more abound
    Majestic Night!

A GREETING.

YE faithful followers of the Muse,
    Ye pensive-soul'd Bohemian crews,
Who study Nature's varying views
    With willing heart,
And for your better portion choose
    The tuneful art.

Ye thoughtful race, who lonely wander
Through Nature's realms and deeply ponder,
Finding your love for her grow fonder
    Each day that flies,
Who know no hope nor wish beyond her
    Sweet mystic ties.

Extol the witching charms of Nature,
Sing descants on each lovely feature
Presented in her grand portraiture
    In earth and sky,
To hymn her praise bid every creature
    With rapture vie.

Sing of her undulating valleys,
The still sweet woods and verdurous alleys,
Sing golden Sol as forth he sallies,
    Like gallant bright,
When Morning floods her orient palace
    In roseate light!

Accept the humble commendation
Of me, a bard of lowly station,
Whose highest hope and aspiration
    Is to attain,
Help'd by the Muse's inspiration,
    Fame's bright domain.

Though captious critics sneer and carp,
Let not their spleen your spirit warp,
But with the music of your harp
    Their murmurs drown;
Stand up to them, and they will sharp
    Leave you alone.

Call on these idle soulless elves
To do some decent work themselves,
To close their spleen-emitting valves,
    And sympathise
With e'en the lowliest soul who delves
    For Honour's prize.

I know no nobler spectacle
Upon which mortal eyes can dwell
Than on some soul who labours well
    To mend his state,
Whose breast Ambition's fire doth swell
    With purpose great.

Though low your lot, and scant your purse,
Though Fortune's frown your pathway curse,
Word-painters of the universe,
    Ye men of rhymes;
In varying strains the themes rehearse
    Of these strange times.

Toil bravely on, each tuneful soul,
Heed not, though adverse billows roll,
With virtue, prudence, self-control,
    Pursue your way,
Unto your aspiration's goal
    The poet's bay!

A SONG.

DEAR bygone days, sweet bygone days,
    How oft, amid our grief and pain,
We backward turn our wistful gaze,
    And would that ye could be again;
Life's morning hours, when woe and care
To our light bosom strangers were.

Dear bygone hours, sweet bygone hours,
    Unto our fancy's eyes ye seem
To represent the faded flowers
    That tell of Summer's golden dream;
Life's fairest hours, so calm and bright
Alas! for ever ta'en their flight.

DEEDS VERSUS CREEDS.

METHINKS it is a small affair indeed
  Whatever be a man's religious creed ;
What matters it what tenets he believes ?
What are these things but merely lifeless leaves ?
While actions are the goodly luscious fruit.

How many men most orthodox to creeds
With firmness hold, and yet are, by their deeds,
As far remote from God-likeness and love
As this our globe from yonder vault above ;
In practice not much higher than the brute !

There's one will say he loves his fellow-man,
And yet, perchance, that very mortal can
Unmov'd behold another in distress,
And him relieve not in his wretchedness,
Though able. What's the value of his creed ?

Another no profession makes at all,
In brief, may be what true believers call
An infidel, yet play the nobler part,
And demonstrate himself of better heart ;
A Christian truly, not in word, but deed.

See we a man considerate and kind,
Of charitable views and breadth of mind,
Upright and manly, honourable, true,
And we behold, alas ! there are so few,
A genuine man, a gem of priceless worth.

Yet here and there such noble souls are found,
True warriors on life's stern battle-ground,
Who prove themselves by many a goodly deed
Superior to mere holders of a creed,
Whose good too often owes to fear its birth.

Above the conflict of contending creeds
The world calls out impatiently for deeds,
It cries aloud :—Ye Christian folk, live out
That love ye talk so fluently about ;
Display the proofs of your sincerity.

We're weary of your inconsistent ways,
Your hollow, vain rhetorical displays;
Why do ye fail so signally to reach
The lofty standard ye so glibly teach ?
Is it a myth your boasted charity ?

O ! would we all but practise what we preach,
By acts of good confirm the good we teach ;
Were we more real, genuine, sincere,
Then would Religion's beauteous light appear
And fill this darken'd world with radiancy.

THE DAY IS DARK AND DREARY.

THE Sun in anger hides his ray,
    The skies are rob'd in sombre gray,
The rain falls fast on hedge and spray ;
        The day is dark and dreary.

Dark is the horizon of my life,
With gathering clouds of sorrow rife,
My breast is full of bitterest strife,
        And all is dark and dreary.

For friends I sigh, and sigh in vain ;
No soul is near to soothe my pain,
Life's load to aid me to sustain,
        Nor comrade kind and cheery.

I yearn to reach that tranquil shade
Where, by Earth's tumults undismay'd,
All calmly rest the peaceful dead,
        No longer sad or weary.

A MIDNIGHT CAT-ASTROPHE.

THE shades of night had settl'd down
  O'er S-w-y Bridge, that rising town
And silence solemn and profound
Rul'd all, above, below, around.

A trio—husband, wife, and son,
Their day's appointed duties done,
All peacefully had sunk to rest,
By Morpheus's weight oppress'd.

Through dreamland's region calm subdue
They sweetly roam'd, while busy Tim
The "wee sma" hours hurried throu
When suddenly there swiftly flew

Through the still house a dread ala
That soon disturb'd their slumber ca
And startl'd Sleep in deep chagrin
Disgusted bolted from the scene.

An awful bumping row they hear
That fills their very soul with fear.
Awakes the echoes of the night.
And all their comfort puts to fligh

Erect in bed the aged pair
Upsprang, while every startl'd hai
Upon each hoary time-worn pate
Stood up like soldiers stiff and stra

Scarce knowing what ought to be
They summon first their only son.
And pour into his youthful ears
The doleful story of their fears.

A member of a fire-brigade,
Of course, he scorn'd to seem afra
Quoth he, just let me see the thi
And soon the scamp will come to

All in their sleeping garb array'd.
A very striking group they made.
The hardy youth his hatchet gra
His sire unto his bosom clasps

His trusty friend, his good " ash plant,"
Well-prov'd in many and many a " rant,"
And, bidding the old dame go first,
They nerve themselves to meet the worst.

Downstairs they creep with bated breath
And trembling feet, while thoughts of death
In varied forms and dreadful pains
Rush swiftly through their heated brains.

Around about they keenly stare,
But nothing meets their vision there
Explanatory of the noise,
And Hope again the bosom buoys.

The youth opin'd they were mista'en,
And mov'd they got to bed again,
Which " motion " well was entertain'd,
And soon their chambers are regain'd.

When lo ! the noise with double force,
Renews itself, and so perforce,
Those stairs they must descend again
To seek the cause of all the din.

Around again with vigilance
In every hole and nook they glance,
Until, despairing, the old " fellar "
Suggests that they should try the cellar.

Accordingly they bend their steps
Into the cellar's gloomy depths,
And, nerving them for mighty blow,
They look round for the lurking foe.

O how they rav'd and stamp'd and swore
When downward gazing, on the floor
The figure of a cat they spy,
At which the irate youth let fly.

It seems, like all the feline ilk,
Pussie was very fond of milk,
And, having come across a jug,
Had tightly wriggl'd in her " mug "

In her keen quest for bovine spoils
And herself fasten'd in the toils;
Then vainly striving to get free,
Had bump'd and hammer'd vigorously,

So causing the alarming noise
That banish'd their nocturnal joys,
That dragg'd them from their cosy bed
And filled their bosoms with such dread.

But, laughing at the harmless scare,
To bed they once again repair,
Right thankful to discover that
'Twas nought more dang'rous than the "cat."

MORAL.

If you would calmly rest at night,
And not be waken'd in a fright,
Take my advice, and be quite sure
You leave no milk jug on the floor.

"FAITHFUL UNTO DEATH."

(During an earthquake that took place in a Russian town in the latter part of the year 1888, a soldier was guarding the Treasury, and, though walls were falling in all around him, he refused to leave his post until ordered to do so by a Sergeant who fortunately had his attention drawn to the position of the gallant fellow.)

UNDYING Fame, upon thy shining scroll
Inscribe the name of this heroic soul!
Bright Glory, weave an amaranthine wreath
To grace his brow, who, faithful unto death,
In peril's hour refus'd to quit his post
And won a place amid that glorious host
Whose noble actions god-like and sublime
Live on until the latest hour of Time.
Such men as he make any nation great,
Add honour to the lowliest estate.
O may he from a generous country's hand
Receive meet guerdon for his valour grand!
And when the dauntless hero's days are o'er,
Kind Angels, waft him to the heavenly shore,
To wear for aye the conqueror's fadeless wreath,
Heaven's crown for all who're faithful unto death.

A CHRISTMAS STORY.

THERE'S trouble on the mighty sea,
   Its bosom heaves tumultuously,
The wind is howling furiously ;
Huge, black clouds scudding o'er the sky
Presage the dreaded tempest nigh ;
From pole to pole red lightning flashes,
The awful thunder rolls and crashes,
Snow-crested billows boil and leap,
Then downward swirl into the deep.
All through the blinding surf and spray
A gallant vessel ploughs her way ;
She reels, she dips, her timbers creak,
As heavy seas athwart her break ;
High on the giddy reeling mast
The reefer sits amid the blast ;
He labours bravely in the gloom,
Unmoved, resign'd unto the doom
That darkly o'er them seems to loom.
Ah ! deem not the bold seaman weak,
If scalding tears bedew his cheek ;
Not for himself his grief has way,
He thinks of dear ones far away :
Again he sees his native village,
The fragrant fields he used to pillage
Of their gems the starry flowers
In boyhood's sunny happy hours.
Sees, too, that dear, familiar spot—
The little ivy-covered cot,
His home, his heart's true resting-place,
His widow'd mother's gentle face ;
And how his life-blood courses warm
As thinks he of another form,
That pretty face and head of gold—
His sweetheart in the days of old.
O shall he gaze on her again,
   And find her to him fondly true,
In pleasure's draught drown all his pain ?
   Thus thinks the reefer ; while the crew
Toil on with all their manhood's might,
And pray for morning's welcome light.

Heaven aid the vessel and her crew,
In mercy guard them safely through
The howling blast, from reef and rock,
Till rests she safely in the dock!
  *   *   *   *

Now turn we to a different scene,
A tiny cottage bright and clean—
Each thing is in its proper place;
No careful eye can fail to trace
That order, tidiness are dear
Unto her heart who dwelleth here.
The little store of homely delf
Display'd upon a humble shelf;
The massive chest of sturdy oak,
That grand old clock, whose sounding stroke
The stillness here for years has broke;
A few old prints upon the walls—
Old country scenes, old-fashion'd halls;
The infant Jesus in a manger,
A little helpless, homeless stranger;
That Sacred Book—its holy page
Youth's wisest guide, the stay of age;
The comfort doubtless of the dame
 Who sits before the cheerful grate,
Gazing into the ruddy flame
 Leaping and dancing so elate.
A gentle white-hair'd dame is she,
 With kindly eye and placid brow;
Old Time hath us'd her tenderly,
 Although stern Winter with his snow
And frosts severe her eyes have seen
Full three-score years and ten I ween;
She sits, a striking illustration
Of meek-ey'd, patient Resignation.
Fond Memory is busy now,
And brings to her remembrance how
'Tis dear, familiar Christmas Eve,
And for awhile the dame doth leave
The present with its care and pain,
And liveth o'er the past again.
Distinctly to her tearful eyes

The well-belovèd form doth rise
Of that kind partner fond and true
From whom no unkind word she knew,
Who long ago was laid to rest
Within Dame Nature's tranquil breast.
That merry-hearted, handsome boy,
Her heart's great hope, her soul's chief joy,
A roamer o'er the restless wave,
A wayward lad, but bold and brave.
She gazes at the vacant chair,
Hallowed by many a tear and prayer,
Dusted and placed for many a year
For him, alas! that came not near.
Thus, while her fancy doth explore
The past, a knock comes at the door,
And enters then a maiden fair,
With eyes of blue and flaxen hair;
A maiden, yet a woman staid,
In modest dignity arrayed.
Beside the dame she takes her seat,
And greeteth her in accents sweet;
A momentary crimson flush
Deepens into a vivid blush,
Then fadeth from her rounded cheek,
As to her friend she thus doth speak:
"O, why should Ralph prefer to roam
The treach'rous deep, 'mid storm and foam,
And never visit once his home
Nor write to you, his mother dear!
My dear lov'd friend, I sadly fear
That he on whom we set such store
Shall never gaze upon us more."
"Nay! nay! my darling, say not so,
For anything we two may know,
Upon his homeward journey now
He may be. Banish from thy brow
That saddened look. If 'tis His will
Who holds the deep, the lofty hill
Within the hollow of His hand,
He'll bring him safely back to land.
That's right, dear; cease your melancholy!

Now fasten up these sprigs of holly!
And here's a bunch of misletoe,
Ah! well I mind, now blush not so,
Long years ago he you did kiss
Beneath a similar piece to this.
Old Christmas comes but once a year,
Then, let us make him welcome, dear!"
The girl, cheer'd by the kindly word,
Speeds the glad task, when lo! is heard
A firm sharp knock, and then another,
And then the joyful cry—"Ah, mother!"
And, all unscathed from Ocean's harms,
Ralph clasps his mother in his arms;
Then turning to his darling Grace,
Enfolds her, too, in his embrace.
No words can tell that mother's joy,
As gazes she upon her boy,
While Grace can only by him stand,
And shyly hold his big brown hand.
The cheerful meal now duly o'er,
Around the cozy fire they draw,
And, with a hand in each of his,
Ralph yields himself to perfect bliss.
Says he, "You long to know, I 'spose,
What has detained me—well, here goes:
'Tis seven years this very day
Since the Stormy Petrel sailed away
With a cargo rich from Plymouth Sound
To Sacramento outward bound.
Well, after a successful run,
We made the port; our task then done,
For merry England we put back,
And soon were on the homeward tack.
But winds contrary overtook us,
From stem to stern they fiercely shook us;
We had to cut away all sail,
And outward carried by the gale,
We drifted rapidly away,
Until on an ill-fated day
Quite suddenly there came a squall
Athwart our craft, and down went all,

Except a few who reach'd an island
  By floating spar and upturn'd boat,
Right thankful but to get on dry land,
  Though uninhabited, remote.
Long dreary years then pass'd away,
We kept on looking day by day;
No welcome sail e'er came our way.
Oh, how we pray'd that one might come,
And bear us safely, quickly home!
At length one day a cheerful shout
Came from our comrades looking out,
Announcing we had been espied,
And there upon the ocean wide
A gallant craft came full in view.
We hail'd her; soon a sturdy crew
Put off to us and quickly landed;
Into the boat soon we were handed;
The captain, like a Briton true,
Did all for us that he could do;
We learn'd that she was homeward bound,
And soon again in Plymouth Sound
We landed, and you see me here.
But now, my lov'd ones, never fear
That I will leave you any more;
I'm going to get a berth ashore
As watchman, or as coastguardsman.
Yes, mother mine, that is my plan;
And when I'm spliced to you, dear Grace,
In this, my own, my native place,
Shall be my resting-place, my home,
No more o'er ocean's depths I'll roam."

*   *   *

Thus sat they out that Christmas Eve,
And laugh'd and talk'd while Hope did weave
Her fabric fair of pleasures sweet,
  Until the pealing bells did greet
The dawning of the happy morn
When Christ, the Prince of Peace, was born.

A PROLOGUE.
"VERBUM SAP."

FAINT heart ne'er won a lady fair,
    So saith the proverb ancient;
Therefore, ye timorous lovers, ne'er
    Be daunted, but in patient,
Stout-hearted confidence abide,
    Assiduously endeavour
To win the maid until the tide
    Of love turn in your favour.

Ye who the steep ascent of Fame
    With eager footsteps climb,
Aspiring to inscribe your name
    Upon the scroll of Time;
Toil on, perchance the kindly Fates
    May to your side be won,
And duly open Fortune's gates
    Unto their struggling son.

Or ye who Learning's classic field
    With pensive eye explore,
Work bravely on until she yield
    Her wealth of precious lore;
Ye may not reach the fair domains
    By any royal way,
But by infinity of pains,
    By labours night and day.

A PROLOGUE.
(Written for an Old English Village Bazaar held at Hanover School early in 1889.)

HANOVER'S friends, list while this lowly rhyme
    Directs your thoughts to good Queen Bess's tim
That period renowned in English story,
When Britain climb'd the bright ascent of glory.
Then Albion, 'neath the ægis of the Tudor,
Securely dwelt and feared not an intruder;
All foreign foes she set at brave defiance,
And led the world in learning, art, and science.
With patriots such as Sydney, Drake, and Raleigh,
The empire grew in peace and plenty daily
Until she reached a height of exaltation

A PROLOGUE

Not yet attained by any other nation;
In town and city toilers dwelt contented,
Or village fair, as this one here presented.

   *   *   *

Mark well the scene replete with quaint old charms—
Ye village inn yclept "Ye Raleigh Arms;"
Hard by, its neighbour grey, yon ancient arch,
Beneath which often times did proudly march
Bold belted knights, stout squires, sturdy yeomen,
In feudal fray to meet their neighbour foemen.
Yon ivy-covered venerable fane,
Resounding oft with prayer and holy strain;
The Stocks, wherein the roving knave or fool
Oft found a seat his vagrant heels to cool;
The Market Cross, where farmers' wives did meet
To sell their poultry, eggs, and butter sweet;
Observe we, too, yon grand manorial hall,
Thrown open wide, alike to great and small.

   *   *   *

And do ye ask, what mean these rustic trains
Of country lasses fair and sturdy swains?
These quaint old shops, whose ample stalls display
Promiscuous and beautiful array
Of fancy wares, all wrought by dexterous hands,
Brought o'er the seas from distant eastern lands,
From Palestine, from grim, grotesque Japan,
Bright offspring of the genius of man?
The reason of this beautiful display
Is, briefly, this, we hold a fair to-day,
And all these goods outspread beneath your eye
Appeal to you to come and freely buy;
With voiceless eloquence they seem to say,
Good people, come and carry us away;
You'll find in us nor blemishes nor flaws,
Remember, too, the goodness of the cause;
In after time, you will feel no regret
That you thus helped to liquidate the debt
Which like an incubus upon our school
So long hath lain. Cold calculating rule
Put on one side, and hand all you can over,
And thus reward the workers at Hanover.

THE CONSTANT HEART.

THERE is a flower that never fades,
  Though others droop and die,
Retaining its enchanting hues
  And fragrance rich for aye :—
The flower of the constant heart—
  O hold this flower dear,
And prize it as the sweetest thing
  Upon this circling sphere !

Within the stately princely hall
  The lovely bloom is found,
In scenes of grandeur, elegance,
  Where luxuries abound ;
But oftener in the lowly soul
  Of some poor child of earth,
'Midst poverty and darkness, shines
  This gem of priceless worth.

BE STILL.

BE still, my troubl'd heart, be still !
  If 'tis thy Heavenly Father's will
That trial, pain, shall be thy lot,
Be strong and patient, murmur not ;
Life's fleeting course will soon be run,
The cross be borne, the crown be won.

What though friend after friend depart—
There is a Friend Whose faithful heart
Will closer than a brother's cleave ;
In Him unfalteringly believe ;
His gracious goodness changeth never ;
Same yesterday, to-day, for ever.

What though the road be long and dark,
And many a stain of error mark
Thy journey o'er the pilgrim way ;
Though often worsted in the fray,
Let this sweet promise cheer thy breast—
He giveth His belov'd rest.

THE BEE.

THE bee that in the summer hour
    Flits restlessly from flower to flower,
Rich nectar from their opening lips
Extracting with delicious sips,
Presents unto the thoughtful mind
A useful lesson to Mankind ;
Which, would they pay to it due heed,
Would some day stand them in good stead.
Observe the toilsome insect's care—
When all is beautifully fair,
Disdaining pleasurable ease,
Employing all its energies,
As if its instinct did foresee
A period of necessity ;
It taketh Fortune at the tide,
When its currents swelling glide ;
With arduous labour doth contrive
To store with luscious sweets its hive.
Perceive, O man ! the lesson great
The industrious bee doth demonstrate ;
Doth not the tiny teacher say :
When shines the sun, then make the hay,
Work on and prosper while you may.
Yes, labour on, remit no pains,
While sickness ne your hand restrains ;
Now in the prime of Manhood's power,
Provide against a future hour ;
To win fair Fortune's cheering smile,
With strenuous efforts bravely toil
Until the sunshine of success
In radiant beams your pathway bless.

A BALLAD.

BE true to me, a lover said,
    As he bent o'er the golden head
Of the fair maiden at his side ;
When far away upon the sea,
Sweet love, wilt thou be true to me ?
I love but thee, the maid replied.

The lover breathes his sad adieu,
Then swiftly o'er the waters blue
Light as a bird the vessel flies;
He goes, nor thinks he to return
Till Fortune's favours he shall earn,
Then will he come and claim his prize.

Long years roll on, he cometh not,
The maiden deems herself forgot,
And to another lends her ear;
Unto another gives her hand
With wealth untold at his command,
Nor thinks of him she once held dear.

A gallant vessel homeward flies;
With triumph gleaming in his eyes
A traveller treads her deck elate;
A few short hours, murmurs he,
And I my beauteous love shall see
Alas! he recks not of his fate.

Unto the maiden he returns.
Full soon the cruel truth he learns;
His joy transform'd to ceaseless pain,
Again he roams o'er Ocean's breast,
To know no more the joy of rest
Till kindly Death shall end life's strain.

THE FLIGHT OF SUMMER.

THE beauties of Summer are fading away,
    We view their departure with grief and dismay,
The varying prospects in sombre garb dight,
Too truly narrate the sad tale of his flight.
The swallows fly homeward, the flowers are few,
The grass is fast losing its emerald hue,
The leaves in thick clusters lie yellow and sere,
And winds softly murmur in cadences drear
As they roam in and out the fast thinning trees;
The songsters no longer their gay minstrelsies
In rapturous glee pour forth with full throat,

But at intervals utter a faint chirping note.
Bird, flower, and leaf in mournful tones say:
Our monarch, bright Summer, is passing away.
Farewell then, grand spirit of beauty and light,
Soon, soon thou wilt be but a memory bright.
The Seasons' gay king, thou hast well play'd thy part,
Hast breath'd sweetest bliss into many a heart,
With a rich floral zone hast encircl'd the scene,
Bath'd meadow, field, woodland in roseate sheen;
In beautiful tints hast thou garnish'd the skies,
And spread in profusion rich food for our eyes;
Hast lighten'd our bosoms and dried up our tears,
With music delicious hast flooded our ears;
Like an angel of good thou hast cheer'd us along,
Dispell'd all our fears, made us hopeful and strong.
But now for a season thou goest away,
And soon shall we groan 'neath Winter's stern sway;
But when Borean blasts shake the forest and glade,
And Earth in her mantle of white is array'd,
We will patiently suffer the cold and the storm,
And long for the time when, rosy and warm,
Again o'er the prospect thou shakest thy wing,
Then farewell, bright Summer, of Seasons the king,

A TRIBUTE.
(In Memory of the Author's niece, Annie Sutcliffe, who died February 19th, 1894.)

METHINKS that Fate ne'er aim'd a crueller blow
Than that swift-wingèd dart that laid thee low,
Dear Maid, array'd in all thy youthful bloom,
Like a fair flower that droops mid Autumn's gloom.
Still, while we shed the tributary tear,
Yet who of us would wish that thou wert here?
If we could only penetrate the haze
That hides the future from our finite gaze,
Perchance we then might think Death was a friend
Who came to thee earth's countless ills to end;
To lead thee to a better land than ours,
To glitt'ring golden streets and fadeless flowers;
Where sorrow, sighing, pain, anxiety
Come not to mar the deep tranquillity;
No sun to shed its overpowering ray,

No fears by night, perplexities by day ;
Where thou shalt ever bathe thy peaceful breast
In the calm ocean of infinite rest.
Thus, Annie, would we wish to think of thee,
As from earth's ills and sin's pollution free ;
Not hopeless thy untimely end deplore ;
Thou art not dead, but only gone before.
And may those who most keenly feel thy loss
With patience and submission bear the cross ;
Think that their loss is thy eternal gain,
Hope, by God's mercy, thee to see again,
And try to say, though sorrow's tempest swell :—
" It is the Lord ; He doeth all things well."

FOR LOVE AND CHIVALRY.
(A Song.)

A WARRIOR resolute and bold,
   Arm'd *cap-a-pie* in burnish'd gold,
Spurs onward to the tourney gay,
Elate and eager for the fray ;
The favours of his ladye fayre
Float bravely on the breezy air,
And with a merry voice sings he :
I fight for Love and Chivalry.

Now in the lists, with lance in rest,
And victory shining on his crest ;
He rushes on the advancing foe,
Soon on the green sward lays him low ;
With breast elate and beaming eyes
Receives from Beauty's hand the prize,
'Midst plaudit loud and revelry,
The bright reward of Chivalry.

With honour crown'd the gallant knight
Rides homeward gaily from the fight ;
His true love from her lattice pane
Descrys him spurring o'er the plain ;
Soon to the warrior's ardent breast
The lovely maid is fondly press'd ;
Dear love, he whispers tenderly,
I've fought for Love and Chivalry.

THE JESTER'S LOVE.

HE was the King's own Jester;
   Amidst the courtly throng
'Twas his to mingle daily,
   With quip, and crank, and song;
To drive away dull-visag'd Care
From noble proud and ladye fayre.

The pun and merry couplet
   Could he command at will,
The graceful tarantella
   Perform with featly skill;
Or keep the table in a roar
With rosy Humour's pleasing lore.

But 'neath that vest of motley
   There was an aching heart,
And in the mirth he call'd forth
   The Jester had no part;
And none knew 'mid the revels gay
The pangs that rent him day by day.

He lov'd a noble maiden,
   A lady highly born;
Ah! vain the hope that ever
   She could his love return;
Look from her altitude sublime
Upon the luckless man of rhyme.

He watch'd her queenly figure
   Move in the mazy dance,
And would have given his best blood
   For but a tender glance;
But little reck'd or heeded she,
Destin'd a great man's bride to be.

Her bridal morn dawns brightly,
   In beauteous robes array'd,
Move belles and gallants knightly,
   A splendid cavalcade,
And just as she became a bride
That very hour the Jester died.

TILL DEATH DO PART.

TWO tender lovers, hand in hand,
    Wander by a rippling stream;
They roam through Pleasure's fairy land,
    Dreaming Love's delicious dream;
I will be true, he fondly cries,
    Doubt me not, my beauteous love,
True as yon sun that gilds the skies,
    Nought from thee my heart can move.

An aged couple, hand in hand,
    Sit before the ruddy blaze;
They've almost reach'd the borderland
    Pilgrims through Life's devious ways;
Through Life's bright morn to its calm eve,
    Faithful they through woe or weal;
Together now they fain would cleave
    In life or death united still.

A LAMENT.

ALAS! what ills the aspiring bard assail
    Who seeks the height Parnassian to scale;
What galling fetters chafe his soaring soul,
What adverse currents o'er him ruthless roll;
What barriers interpose themselves between
Him and the goal his hopes are centred in!
Spending his manhood in laborious days;
His nights in dreams of amaranthine bays;
The proud man's scorn, the worldling's cynic sneer,
Malignity's keen thrust, and Envy's carp and jeer;
A scant-lin'd purse, friends few and far between,
Gay gleams of hope, and disappointments keen;
Inconstant friends, the critic's cruel flailing,
Tormenting doubts, misgivings dire of failing;
All these, and more too numerous to name,
Obstruct the path of those who seek for fame,
In Glory's temple bright an honour'd niche to claim.
As loftiest heights encounter fiercest gales,
While calm and tranquil rest the lowly vales,
They who would tread the higher paths of life

Have oft to forge their way through fiercest strife.
But as the warrior views with ardent eyes
The foe advance, and feels his courage rise,
So the true bard, as he surveys his foes,
His inborn pluck proportionately grows
The obstacles to meet that would his way oppose.
The artist, too, who really loves his art,
Though doubts and fears betimes assail his heart,
Before his vision keeps his grand ideal,
And labours on with never-flagging zeal.
Let genius in a man but have its root,
Be it but tended well, the goodly fruit
In time it must inevitably yield,
As harvests bless the cultivated field.
On then, my friends! O be ye undismay'd!
What e'er the power against your souls arrayed.
As when dark clouds disperse with swiftest pace
Before the beams of Sol's resplendent face,
So shall your genius, with its brilliant light,
Disperse your foes, make all your pathway bright.
Let nothing then your upward flight retard,
In due time Labour wins its fair reward.

CARISSIMMA.

AH, dearest one, my hope, my life,
   How dark this world would be,
One dismal scene of pain and strife
   Were I bereft of thee;
Wealth, rank, and power have no charms
   To call forth my desires;
To rest me in thy snowy arms
   My heart alone aspires.

Thy beauteous hair, each silky tress,
   My pure, my precious gold,
Thy tender thought, thy kind caress,
   My treasury untold;
To breathe the same sweet air as thee
   Is rich, is perfect bliss;
Thy love can fill with radiancy
   A darken'd world like this.

THE TALE OF LIFE.

A TENDER bud on life's great tree,
The helpless little babe we see,
Reposing in its tiny cot,
The while the eulogistic note
Ascending from admiring friends
The infant's opening hours attends.

A merry-hearted little boy ;
No greater cares his thoughts employ
Than the dear-lov'd and trivial toy ;
A spirit frolicsome and gay
Sporting through life's golden day :
Dreaming oft delicious dreams,
Wandering by silvery streams ;
Murmuring tunefully between
Sloping banks of tender green ;
Gazing at the azure sky,
Chasing the gay butterfly ;
Pillaging the scented bowers,
Bearing home the pretty flowers,
While the mother's heart doth joy
To behold her darling boy.

The sturdy active vigorous youth
Bounding o'er life's pathway smooth,
Stranger unto pain and care,
Hope presenting pictures fair ;
Life one pleasant prospect seems
Deck'd in gorgeous solar beams :
Drinking draughts of purest joy,
Nought to trouble or annoy,
Fancy floating unconfin'd ;
Life's sweet seed-time when the mind
Opes itself unto impression,
Ere the fever fire of passion
Hath hardened with its lurid blaze—
O precious, priceless youthful days !

Advancing then in Nature's plan,
Behold we now the full-grown man ;
An earnest being, toiling, striving,

Restless, scheming, and contriving;
Navigating life's rough sea,
Ofttime sailing perilously,
The waves of ruin wild and dark
Threatening his fragile barque;
At times the beams of Fortune's sun
Brightly shine his pathway on;
The lover, husband, then the father;
Around him little children gather,
Clinging like tendrils round his heart,
Nerving his arm to play its part,
The music of their simple prattle,
In the world's incessant battle
Thrills him as ringing clarion call
Stirreth the warrior's ardent soul.
So he labours hard and long,
Singing Pleasure's cheery song,
Mourneth now in accents drear
Darksome dirges of despair;
Notes of joy and chords of pain
Blend in Life's mysterious strain.

Then with the lagging step of age
He traverseth Life's closing stage
Wreath'd in hiemal darkness drear,
Perchance of all that life held dear
Bereft; the cheering hopes that lighted,
Gone, like the flowers in winter blighted;
No longer glad his aged ear
The accents of his lov'd ones dear;
Like some old tree that bends its form
Beneath the fury of the storm,
He bendeth low while life doth shed
Its winds and tempests on his head,
Until beneath the verdant sod
He mingles with his native clod.

And thus the tale of life goes on—
A meteor flash—and then 'tis gone,
A strain of music rich and rare
That dies upon the empty air;
A tender flower, no sooner blown,

Than sinks it in some pathway lone.
Of all the tales from ancient books
By hermits read in peaceful nooks
Most wondrous is the tale of life—
Bright peaceful hours, dark days of strife,
Gay peals of laughter, sorrow's tears,
Hope's beaming sunshine, gloomy fears,
Clangour gay of wedding bells,
Dreary dirge of funeral knells,
Perplexity, uncertainty,
Care, restlessness, anxiety,
Dark clouds with care and sorrow rife,
Make up the total sum of life.

MY TRUE LOVE.

MY true love she is fair;
   No lady in the land,
   However rich and grand,
With my love can compare.

My true love she is kind—
   A softer simpler heart,
   More free from guileful art
You surely cannot find.

My true love she is poor,
   But with her charms to grace
   My lowly dwelling-place,
I ask for nothing more.

My true love clings to me
   Through good report or ill,
   Come weal or woe, I've still
Her love and sympathy.

My true love she is dead.
   Upon her earthy pillow,
   Beneath the weeping willow
They laid her golden head.

And I am left alone;
   The world is cold and hollow,
   O that I soon might follow
Where my true love is gone!

THE LADY OF THE LAND.

A LOVELY lady of the land,
  Living in a mansion grand;
Beautiful and chaste was she
As ever mortal eye did see;
A figure of exquisite mould,
Her head adorned with coils of gold,
Brightly shone her eyes of blue;
Ah, few were they, and very few,
Who could the witchery withstand
Of this proud lady of the land!

Noble ones of high degree
Sigh'd for her, but hopelessly;
Cupid aim'd his darts in vain;
Heedless of their heart's deep pain,
She would tell them laughingly
She preferr'd her liberty;
None would she of nuptial bond.
Then her high-born lovers fond
Could never hope to win the hand
Of this cold lady of the land.

But she met her fate one day;
A gallant youth came in her way,
And her proud heart had to own
At last had come the favour'd one;
But she would not bend her pride—
Broken-hearted from her side
To foreign lands he went away,
And falling foremost in the fray,
He perish'd by a foeman's hand,
All through the lady of the land.

But this lady of the land,
Wealthy, beautiful, and grand,
Had to feel Love's ceaseless pain,
And she wished, but all in vain,
He would come again to woo.
Oh, he should not vainly sue!
But he came not day by day,
And pin'd she gradually away;
Then sank 'neath Death's unsparing hand
The beauteous lady of the land.

THE JESTER.

I'M a jester by trade,
  In motley array'd ;
With my bauble and bells
I hold forth to the swells,
I've quips and I've cranks
And comical pranks ;
In satirical rhymes
I hit off the times,
  I dwell on each foible and folly;
Mirth follows my track,
For I've hit on the knack
  How to always appear to be jolly.

Though the keen tooth of sorrow
  Is gnawing my heart,
Smiling visage I borrow,
  And practise the art
Of always presenting a merry outside
To the people around me whatever betide.

I can dance at your command
Tarantella, saraband ;
Rhyme you triplet, quartet, couplet,
Clothe my Muse in homely doublet ;
Or in vesture patrician,
At home in high or low position ;
I'm full of funniosities ;
Sparkling pun atrocities
Audaciously I perpetrate ;
Or with mien demure, sedate,
Like a cleric learn'd I prate
Of varying theologies,
Of bursaries and colleges ;
With my caustical wit
Make the "palpable hit ; "
With solemn sonorosity
Dose you with philosophy,
Tricks of verbal jugglery
Rattle off like A B C—
A model of ability,
Of versatile fertility.

THE JESTER.

In the halls of the great,
Mid the grandeur of state,
   The spirit, the soul of the revels;
Oft when trial, grief, care,
Love, pain, hate, and despair
   Rage within me like so many devils.

'Mid the gay rustic crowd,
How the laugh rings aloud
   At my jokes and my antics so funny,
When oft tortures I feel,
Wounds that no balm can heal,
   No patronage, favour, or money.

The plaything, the scorn
Of the loftily born,
   A target at which would-be wits
May practise their skill,
While oft the gay belle
   Laughs loud at their salleys and hits.

O ye damozels fair,
And gay gallants, beware!
   Lest the jester his satires do fling;
With the edge of my dart
I can pierce each proud heart,
   As the fowler the bird on the wing.

In a staid party humdrum,
The solemn conundrum
   Propounding with proper decorum,
A dull mess of pottage
Of dry anecdotage
   With humility setting before 'em.

With a smile on my face
I endure while his Grace
   Drawls forth a long Latin quotation;
Then I ope the scant store
Of my classical lore,
   For each prosy divine's delectation.

Then the fool must be clever,
And never, no never,
  Be dull, flat, or mopish, downhearted;
His mirth must not know
An ebb in its flow,
  Or soon on his way he'll be started.

His wit must be light,
His satire be bright,
  Coruscations meteorologic,
His knowledge of law
Sans error or flaw,
  Convincing and cutting his logic.

Like Yorick of yore,
The house in a roar
  To keep's his peculiar function,
Or my Lord will look black,
Maybe give him the "sack"
  Without ruth or the slightest compunction.

Thus through Life's little day
Goes the fool on his way,
  Strange admixture of mirth, melancholy,
And the world much may learn,
Had it eyes to discern,
  From the "Merryman" and from his folly.

THE TALE OF LOVE.

WHEN mellow Evening's placid beam
   Bath'd meadow, hill, and slumb'ring stre
I wander'd with my own true love
Athrough the stilly verdant grove;
I gaz'd upon her ripening charms,
And press'd her fondly in my arms,
Oft tasting in delicious sips
Rich nectar from her ruby lips,
As 'neath Diana's glances pale
I softly breath'd love's tender tale.

O beauteous love, earth's purest joy,
Sweet bliss unmingl'd with alloy ;
How dark and drear this world would be
Without thy lovely radiancy !
What visions fair dost thou unfold,
How many a heart like marble cold
Hath melted 'neath thy fervent ray,
And bow'd to thy resistless sway !
The diamond's dazzling ray must pale
Before the light of love's sweet tale.

Our vows we fondly did renew,
The flatterer Hope fair pictures drew
Of joys to come in future days ;
The world unto our sanguine gaze
Seem'd as a garden wond'rous fair,
With luscious fruits and flowers rare ;
The memory of that blissful night
Oft fills me with a deep delight,
When 'neath the beam of Dian pale
I whisper'd Love's delicious tale.

DRIVE THEM BACK OVER THE WATER.

WHEN war's ringing clarion the sailor invites
    To action, no dangers appal him.
For the heart of the patriot ever delights
    To be found where'er duty may call him ;
As the shots thickly fly, his courage soars high,
    At home 'mid the din and the slaughter ;
Cries each bold jolly Jack, Now, my lads, drive them back,
    Drive them back over the water.

Our ancestors bled in the brave days of old,
    And won us a name great in story ;
Then pass'd down the order to us to uphold
    The traditions of Albion's glory ;
To our charge ever true, our best will we do,
    Let the foe come from every quarter ;
And again and again shall they try, but in vain,
    We'll drive them back over the water.

TARRY NOT.

O TARRY not, my peerless love,
    Beneath thy lattice pane I wait;
Come, and together we will rove
    Down by the little wicket gate—
The dear familiar place of tryst—
    Where first we told Love's tender tale,
Where first thy blushing face I kiss'd
    Beneath Diana's glances pale.

O darksome are the bluest skies,
    Dull Nature's robe of sweetest green,
If the bright sunshine of thine eyes
    Illumine not the mundane scene;
Arise, O come, my life, my queen,
    I live not until thou art near;
No clouds of earth can intervene,
    If thou, my orient, appear.

MEMORY.

O MEMORY! sweet mysterious thing,
    Thy reproducing power I sing.
Led by thy wonder-working hand,
How oft into the Past's dim land
Our busy thoughts long journeys make,
And, full of wistful longing, take
A tender glance at bygone times.
In fancy oft, like silvery chimes,
Soft, dulcet-like, distinctly clear,
There fall upon our listening ear
The tones of many a dear-lov'd voice,
That erstwhile made our heart rejoice.
Soft whispers of some darling one—
Who from Life's chequer'd scene hath gone.
How oft thy beauteous light imparts
Sweet balm unto our wounded hearts;
As through thy telescope we gaze
And snatch from glimpses of past days
A momentary sweet relief
From present trials, present grief.

MEMORY.

We wander by the golden shore
Of thy fair ocean, and explore
Again with busy eager gaze
Sweet Childhood's sunny, happy days.
We see again the friends so true
In whose companionship we drew
Sweet draughts of purest happiness,
Dear friends, heaven-given our souls to bless,
The future to our ardent gaze
With Hope's bright glory all ablaze.
Alas! alas! how very few
Have realis'd the hopes that threw
Such golden glamour o'er the way
In young Life's roseate-tinted day!
How many sadden'd hearts have prov'd
What 'tis to see all hope remov'd,
Their glowing visions all dispell'd,
More flimsy, aërial structures fell'd
By the relentless, powerful hand
Of conquering Time, who waves his wand
And works such changes in Life's scene.
Victorious Death, with sickle keen,
Hath made such desolating gaps
In love's bright circle; now, perhaps,
The soft, unbidden tear may rise
And dim the brightness of the eyes
That rest upon this lowly page,
As visions of a father sage
Come clearly up before the mind.
Ye tender tears! flow unconfin'd;
Sweet are the tears that owe their birth
To memories of a father's worth.
How sweet the task to fondly trace
The bending form and kind grave face
Of her who, in our tender years,
Sooth'd all our pains and calm'd our fears,
And softly woo'd for us sweet rest
Upon her tender, faithful breast;
Who closely watch'd our gradual growth
From infancy to vigorous youth,
Striving with counsels kind and wise

To set before our youthful eyes
Fair Wisdom's sacred, pleasant road,
And, by her bright example, shew'd
What 'twas to trust in God always
Through brief Life's fleeting, changeful days.
What tongue can tell, what measure prove
The greatness of a mother's love?
Its ocean depths what line can sound?
No better friend on earth is found.
How oft amid our doubts and fears,
Her soft tones fall upon our ears,
Lessening Life's dull weary strain,
Telling of union again
On yonder tranquil shining shore
When our pilgrimage is o'er.
O come fond Memory! oft again,
And lighten up this earthly plain;
Oft when at close of toilsome day,
Our aching frames to rest we lay;
When all-pervading, queenly night,
In sable robe enfolds the light,
Reveal each dear familiar scene—
The things and places that have been.

HE HAS GONE.

HE has gone, we have parted in anger,
   He has left me in wounded pride,
And a tender word would have recall'd him
   With swiftness again to my side;
But pride my affection o'ermaster'd,
   And that soft word, alas! was not said;
But, without a farewell, he has left me,
   And all life's sweet sunshine is fled.

He said that I never had lov'd him—
   Ah me! how the cruel word went through
My heart like the point of a dagger;
   O darling one, if you but knew
How sad is my heart, and how lonely,
   How dear, how unspeakably dear
Thou art, and must ever be to me—
   I would give all the world wert thou near.

LIFE'S INEQUALITIES.

To some this world's a garden fair,
    Where flowers and fruit luxuriant grow;
Across their pathway pain and care
    No soul-bedark'ning shadows throw.

To some it is a sterile field,
    A dreary unproductive waste,
And what scant measure it doth yield
    Is ofttimes bitter to the taste.

To some it is a ceaseless fight
    'Gainst difficulties—adverse bands,
Where oft 'tis seen that might, not right,
    Triumphant at the issue stands.

While, undisturb'd by strife's alarms,
    Some hold an even, tranquil way,
And lovely Peace, in all her charms,
    Sheds o'er their path her mellow ray.

To some 'tis like an azure sky,
    Unchequer'd by a speck of grey;
No darksome clouds of sorrow nigh,
    But one serene, unbroken day.

To others, like a funeral pall
    Appears the aspect of life's sky,
That shuts out from the prospect all
    That's pleasant, cheering to the eye.

To some it is a stormy deep;
    Huge billows leap, with foaming crest,
And adverse winds in fury sweep—
    A deep, perpetual unrest.

To others 'tis a placid lake,
    Athwart whose bosom silvery clear
In joy and ease their way they take,
    Without a doubt or thought of fear.

In fair Fortuna's chariot bright
    Some lightly bowl along life's way,
And hail with breast serene and light
    The joys of each recurring day;

While others through the gloomy vale
  Of poverty limp worn and sore;
Misgivings dire their hearts assail,
  The wolf stands ever at the door.

Ask we the question, why it is
  Such inequalities there be?
Why some should have so much of bliss;
  Others so much of misery?

That question never will receive
  Its answer here; we may not know
The why and wherefore till we leave
  This scene of mingling joy and woe.

Whate'er our rank, our portion here;
  Whate'er of good or ill we have;
With death distinctions disappear;
  We all are equal in the grave.

Just as through various channels flow
  The streams that swell the ocean vast,
From mountain high, through valley low,
  And reach the same great bourne at last;

So borne on Time's resistless tide,
  Life's serried masses onward sweep,
Through toil and want, or pomp and pride,
  Into eternity's great deep.

THE EMIGRANT SHIP.

THE good ship leaves the busy quay,
    Laden with a precious freight,
She rapidly puts out to sea,
  With swelling canvas, snowy white,
Bearing within her ample breast
  A little world of doubts and fears,
Of anxious hearts in eager quest
  Of brighter days in distant spheres.

THE EMIGRANT SHIP.

In thoughtful, tearful groups they stand
   Upon the stately vessel's deck,
Gazing intently, till the land
   Fades in the distance like a speck;
The dire reflection makes them sad
   That their dimmed eyes shall look in vain,
When but a few short hours are fled,
   For their dear-lov'd land again.

The manly youth, the pride, the hope
   Of some poor lonely widow'd heart,
Goes forth with life's stern facts to cope
   In fertile field or crowded mart.
Before his eager, sanguine eyes
   Fond Fancy spreads a picture fair,
Painted in Hope's most brilliant dyes,
   And pleasure banishes dull care.

The beauteous maid, leaving her home,
   Drawn gently by Love's silken chain,
In simple trustfulness to roam
   The blue expanse of ocean main,
To meet upon some distant strand,
   The choice of her fond faithful heart,
And, bound by holy nuptial band,
   To constant cleave till death shall part.

That erring one, in deep disgrace,
   Poor exile from his native land,
Wearing upon his careworn face
   The felon's dark degrading brand;
Retreating wisely from temptations,
   So he, perchance, may earn again,
In new scenes, new associations,
   A place 'midst honourable men.

The honest-hearted labouring band,
   Sad children of adversity,
Unable longer to withstand
   The pressure of necessity,
Seeking with earnest, anxious eyes
   A chance in some less crowded sphere,
To win 'neath more propitious skies
   The right to live denied them here.

Though dangers manifold and dread
    May hover darkly o'er their way,
Though they perhaps, in watery bed
    May rest ere dawns another day;
Bright hope each bosom up doth buoy—
    Trustful and patient, strong and brave,
With whispers sweet of coming joy,
    When they have cross'd the heaving wave.

Kind heaven befriend these wand'ring souls,
    O rest them calmly in His care
Whose matchless might the deep controls,
    And rules the boundless realms of air.
Soon may they all in safety gain
    The haven where they fain would be,
Find home and friends beyond the main,
    And dwell in calm security.

MY LADY SLEEPS.

MY Lady sleeps; kind angels, guard her
    Through the night's dark solemn hour;
Here will I stand, her faithful warder,
    Till on hill, and stream, and flower
Bright Aurora's roseate ray
Rest, presaging golden day.

My lady sleeps, my dearest treasure
    Safely keep, ye spirits fair!
Morning light can bring no pleasure,
    Dawn it e'er so brightly fair,
Till my lov'd one, safe from harms,
Glad my eyes with her sweet charms.

Phœbe gilds her snowy pillow
    With her softest purest ray;
Philomela on the willow
    Breathes forth Love's delicious lay;
Angel guards, my love defend,
Sweetest dreams her sleep attend.

SLEEP, CALMLY SLEEP.

SLEEP, calmly sleep, poor child of sorrow !
    Sweet be thy dreams,
Fond fancies whispering of a to-morrow
    Ting'd with the beams
Of Hope's most radiant, roseate light ;
A future fair, all prosperous and bright.

Sleep, calmly sleep, O wanderer weary !
    Forget thy woes ;
Forget life's journey-path, so long and dreary,
    Its battle throes ;
In Lethe's water steep thy wearied brain,
And snatch a respite brief from all thy care and pain.

Sleep, sailor, sleep ! although thy pillow
    The restless deep,
The ceaseless music of the heaving billow
    Thy senses steep ;
Secure and tranquil on thy rude bed lie,
Beneath His watchful care Who rules the sea and sky.

Sleep, soldier, sleep ! the cannon's rattle
    Will thee ere long
Awaken ; and the horrid din of battle,
    Where perils throng
Shall summon thee to meet thy country's foes ;
Strength for the coming fray find thou in deep repose.

Sleep, calmly sleep, O orphan desolate !
    Safe in His care
Whose strong right hand shall make thy pathway straight ;
    From every snare
He will deliver, be with thee in distress,
And prove Himself a father unto the fatherless.

Sleep, softly sleep, O baby innocent !
    A shining band
Of angels fair, on guardian mission sent,
    Around thee stand,
Enfolding thee within their pinions white,
That no ill dreams molest thy slumbers pure and light.

Sleep, calmly sleep, ye sick who languish
    On beds of pain ;
Whose journey-way lies through the path of anguish ;
    Soon shall ye gain
That blissful sphere—that sinless, painless land,
Where the redeemèd in immortal vigour stand.

O gentle sleep, worn Nature's faithful friend,
    In mercy given
The ravages of toil and thought to mend ;
    Sweet gift of Heaven !
All praise be unto Him Whose tender care bestows.
This inestimable boon—the blessing of repose.

THE LOVERS.

TWO lovers stand at a cottage door
    To breathe their sad adieux,
The moon beams bright o'er hill and moor
    And silvers the falling dew ;
Farewell ! farewell ! my beauteous love,
    He whispers tenderly,
By yonder mellow moon above,
    I will return to thee.

Ah me, the weeping maid replied,
    How dark my lot will be
When thou my love, my hope, my pride,
    Art on the rolling sea !
And when the tempest's dreaded power
    Sweeps fiercely o'er the lea,
My trembling heart will sink and cower,
    O stay, my love, with me !

Two lovers stand at a cottage door,
    Long years have roll'd away,
Again the moon bathes hill and moor
    With her soft silvery ray ;
As in his arms the maiden fair
    Nestles right lovingly,
She whispers : Heaven has heard my prayer
    And brought thee back to me.

THE IDIOT LAD.

WAND'RING low, and wand'ring high,
With pallid face, " lac-klustre eye,"
Peering round with vacant stare,
Unkempt and matted his long hair
Black as the raven's glossy wing,
Now talking loud, 'non whispering,
A poor half-witted hapless thing;
Oft on the air his piteous moan
And mirthless tuneless laugh were borne
From blushing morn to dusky gloaming
From place to place incessant roaming;
A sight to make the thoughtful sad
Was simple Tom, the idiot lad.

His mother, a fair rustic maid,
By trusting love to ill betray'd,
Into our peaceful village stray'd
One day, and begg'd that she might rest,
And the sweet baby at her breast;
She said she'd travell'd many a mile,
And needed sorely rest awhile;
Touch'd by her looks and tone of grief,
The neighbours proffer'd her relief;
Good Widow Robins bade her stay
With her until her journey way
She should be able to resume;
The kind old soul her humble room
Shar'd with her sorrow-stricken guest,
And bade the weary wand'rer rest.
But ere the blush of Morning's light
Had tipp'd with gold the lofty height,
Her weary spirit took its flight,
And when Sol's earliest rays were shed,
They shone upon the stranger dead.

Then the neighbours fill'd with pity
For the tender orphan pretty
Left to tread Life's path alone,
Took to the helpless little one;
They undertook to bring it up,
That while they had a bite or sup

THE IDIOT LAD.

The child should share. Time roll'd along.
Into a lad active and strong
The orphan grew, alas! sad truth,
A hopeless idiot from his youth.

The name of Tom they gave the boy;
The farmers found him oft employ
To run on errands, help with hay,
And glean when yellow harvest lay
A waving field of golden corn.
He was a strange uncanny child,
Now quiet, tractable, and mild,
Anon impetuous and wild;
Now setting off for days together,
Regardless he of wind and weather,
Roaming the dreary solitude,
The lonely dell, the pathless wood;
Climbing with glee the lofty height,
Watching the birds till lost to sight,
Roaming through many a fragrant bower,
Culling full many a strange wild flower,
And weaving many a chaplet fair
To deck some maiden's golden hair.
Ofttimes beside the straying stream
The hapless lad would lie and dream—
In visions sweet his mother dear
A beauteous angel would appear,
Her face illum'd with holy joy,
Smiling upon her lonely boy.
Awaking with a bitter sigh
To find no tender mother nigh,
Then to the village he would come;
A welcome warm in every home
Awaited him, for all were glad
To see again the idiot lad.
The little children ran to him;
He'd humour them in varying whim.
He'd help the tiny babe to walk,
Smile at its first attempts to talk,
Join in the older children's play,
Go with them oft on holiday
On many a nutting expedition;

THE IDIOT LAD.

So generous his disposition
That the last morsel he would share;
The wearied youngster homeward bare
Upon his shoulders broad and strong,
Crooning some strange uncanny song.
Often at night when all was still,
Seated upon some lofty hill,
Poor Tom would gaze with wistful eye
Upon the still and solemn sky;
When asked by us in calmer day
Why thus he wander'd, he would say:
" No ill can come by day or night
" To do me harm; poor Tom's all right."
One day, while playing by the stream,
The lad was startled by a scream,
And turning round, saw with dismay
The torrent carrying away
The Squire's darling little daughter.
Swift as a dart, into the water
With exclamation loud he sprung,
Grasp'd the poor child, who tightly clung
To him till safely on the land
He plac'd his charge. With liberal hand
The Squire repay'd our hero grand,
And all the village were so glad
And proud of Tom, the idiot lad.

E'er busy Time whose ceaseless range
Works in our world such wondrous change,
Sweeping away the proud, the great,
The learn'd and the illiterate,
And many a mighty dynasty
Into Oblivion's deep wide sea,
Brought to our peaceful village woe,
For ruthless Death whose cruel blow
Or soon or late must lay us low
To bear away poor orphan Tom
With slow yet certain steps did come.
The deadly symtoms of his sway
Our eyes had mark'd for many a day—
The hectic flush upon the cheek,
His failing steps and utterance weak,

The racking cough that rent his frame,
Shew'd the inexorable claim
All owe poor Tom was doom'd to pay.
Without a tremor of dismay
He felt the awful change draw near,
And strange to say, his mind more clear
Became. The children soft did tread,
And stood around his dying bed,
While fast the pitying teardrops fell
O'er the dear friend they lov'd so well.
Then Tom with his poor failing voice
Bade them the rather all rejoice
That the kind angels soon would come
To bear his peaceful spirit home.
So gradually from day to day
'Twixt heav'n and earth he ling'ring lay;
At times his busy mind seem'd straying,
And he would fancy he was maying,
Or wand'ring by the winding stream;
His eyes would brighten with a gleam,
And he would murmur with delight:
" Where'er I be, by day or night,
" No harm can come; poor Tom's all right."
With tearful eyes and downcast head
We stood in silence round his bed;
We caught the last few words he said.
Raising his poor thin hand on high,
He pointed with delighted cry:
" See ! See ! My mother's standing there.
" Do you not see her ? O, how fair ! "
Then fell his arms across his breast,
And Tom the idiot was at rest.

OUR GIFTS.

WE are not gifted all alike,
    To each is severally given
His talents, opportunities
    By the will of All-wise Heaven.

OUR GIFTS.

To one is giv'n the gift of song,
    The noble, elevating power
That smoothes the wrinkl'd brow of Care
    And lightens up the festive hour.

Another wields with skilful grace
    The pencil of the artist true,
And with facility portrays
    The lovely face, the pleasing view.

Another plies with signal power
    The ready writer's magic pen,
Pleading with moving eloquence
    The varying interests of men.

This one 's endow'd with ready wit,
    With Intuition's eagle glance,
That sees, and seizes instantly
    Advantages of timely chance,

While that man has the wisdom deep,
    And penetrating gaze to pierce
The veil of mystery that enshrouds
    The secrets of the universe.

Another an exhaustless fund
    Of humour hath his soul within,
With pathos sweetly interspers'd,
    And mingling mirth and tears doth win.

Another the rich tuneful gift
    Of poetry, whose sacred fire,
Excelling learning, science, art,
    To varying measures tunes his lyre.

While firmly in the tender heart
    Of one, perchance to fame unknown,
That noblest, grandest gift of all—
    Blest Charity—hath rear'd her throne.

And all these goodly gifts are given
    To cheer the changeful lot of man,
And shed a beauteous radiance
    Athwart this life's allotted span.

THE OLD YEAR.

OLD year, thou'rt drawing to a close;
  We stand to watch thy dying throes;
We see thee draw each labour'd breath,
Like mortal at the point of death.
A few more hours and thou'lt be gone,
Thy labours o'er, thy journey done--
Into Oblivion's dark clime
Borne hence by hoary-headed Time,
Upon whose current swift and strong
Man's finite race is borne along
Until the Archangel's trumpet roar
Proclaimeth "time to be no more."
Yet, e'er thou quittest our poor sphere,
Fain would I whisper in thine ear
The tribute of the deep regard
Of me, an unknown nameless bard.
For thou hast been to me a friend,
And gratitude could ne'er thy end
Indifferently, coldly view.
How closely have I watch'd thee through
Thy circling way! I saw thy form,
And met thee with a greeting warm,
When first a little helpless child
Thou on this roving planet smil'd.
I mark'd thy growth as week by week
Rude tempests brush'd thy infant cheek,
When blasts hiemal shook the plain,
And Nature, bound in captive chain,
Moan'd piteously until, as Spring,
Thou didst a bright deliverance bring—
Bedizen'd as a lovely maid
In beauteous garb of light and shade.
Again the birdling's thrilling song
On ether mild was borne along,
Transform'd earth again was seen
In her fair robe of vernal green,
And on the trees, erstwhile so sere,
The buds of promise did appear.
Then I thy grander glories view'd
When Summer bright bath'd hill and wood

In radiant sheen, and o'er the plain
Was hung a flowery-scented chain,
And golden-visag'd Sol was seen
Presiding o'er the gladsome scene.
Then, too, I mark'd with thoughtful eye,
As swiftly onwards thou didst fly,
Fair Summer's ripen'd beauties fade
Until at length thou wert array'd
In Autumn's vest of soberer hues—
When deeper shades and sombre views,
The yellow leaf and failing light
Told eloquently Summer's flight.
Then Winter with his arrows keen
Came in to dominate the scene.
Alas! array'd in cold and gloom,
Old year, thou sinkest to thy tomb.

MY LOVE.

MY love she is a maiden fair
   Whose deep blue eyes, light golden hair,
And slender form so frail and slight
Enthral me with a giant's might;
Led willing captive at her pleasure,
She is my heart's best, dearest treasure.

My love is kind, her heart as true
As yon ethereal azure blue
That richly decks the summer skies;
Love beams within her melting eyes;
Secure from all Earth's vain alarms
I rest me in her snowy arms.

My love's a maid with heart as brave
As his who treads the restless wave,
Or warrior's who the battle scene
Surveys with bosom strong, serene;
And come what may, what ills betide,
She aye will tarry by my side.

FANCYLAND.

I LOVE to gaze upon the night
   When all is mantl'd in repose,
And over moor and mountain height
   The moon her chasten'd radiance throws.

The countless silvery stars that glow
   Like jewels in a robe of blue
I love to see as on they go
   Sailing the aërial ocean through.

How beauteous is the rural scene
   In all its peaceful solitude,
The slumbering stream, the meadow green,
   The solemn venerable wood!

And, gazing up into the night,
   With fancy's dreamy eye I see
A realm most beauteous and bright,
   A land of deepest mystery.

O wondrous world of fancy-land!
   My weary soul I fain would rest
Upon thy mystic airy strand,
   And quit this region of unrest.

Bright faces on me seem to smile,
   They speak to me in accents kind:
Poor mortal, wait a little while
   In patient trust; be strong, resign'd.

In this fair world are no false friends,
   No double-minded, insincere,
Who use you but to serve their ends
   Taint not this purer atmosphere.

Alas! oft with a bitter sigh
   I quit the realm of beauteous dreams
To face the stern reality
   Of this poor round of sordid schemes.

O wondrous thought! This world of ours
   Might be a region fair and grand,
Would we employ for good the powers,
   The varying gifts at our command.

THE AUTHOR'S ASPIRATION.

To your kind query, worthy friend,
   As to the hope, the aim, and end
  I have in view,
With breast elate and kindling eye,
Unhesitating my reply
   Make I to you:

The clouds that o'er my lowly fate
So darkly lour to dissipate
   I mean to try,
And up Parnassus's steep side,
But once I gain a single stride,
   Climb by and by.

I know that better men than I
Have at the same game had a try,
   And sadly fail'd;
I also know that others, too,
Have bravely fought the battle through,
   And have prevail'd.

Although to aid my lofty aim
Fair Learning's wealth I may not claim
   Of classic lore,
Than Nature's spirit-stirring fire,
The tuneful Muse to sweep my lyre,
   I ask no more.

Though difficulties throng the road
That leads to Fortune's bright abode,
   And skies are black;
Though means are scant, and friends be **few**,
My arduous journey I'll pursue,
   And ne'er look back.

Though adverse billows fiercely roll
Their chilling currents o'er my soul,
   My goal I'll keep
Right constantly before my view
Until the toiler's guerdon due
   My efforts reap.

THE TRUE POLITICIAN.

TRUE-BORN Englishmen should never
   Be the abject servile minions
Of any man how wise or clever;
   But should hold their own opinions,
Bas'd on Justice, Truth, and Reason,
   Though the advocates of " party "
Dub it " heresy " and " treason,"
   If they fail to give a hearty
Vote for any every scheme
   By some leading light propounded,
Any vain Utopian dream
   On imagination founded.
A man should act up to his own,
   Not another's sense of justice;
Better far to stand alone
   In manly honesty than trust his
Conscience to the custody
   Of some autocratic leader;
His own conviction aye should be
   His only, his acknowledged leader,
Whose strong persuasive eloquence
   Aye should win his leal allegiance;
Fearlessness of consequence,
   Deep disdain for mere expedience;
Honesty in all his dealings,
   Purity in all transactions,
Deaf to sinister appealings
   Of corrupt dishonest factions;
Contempt for the majority
   When an unjust path pursuing,
Giving the priority
   To Honour's dictates, never ruing.
Let right be though the heavens descend,
   Should the true man's motto be,
Though it cost him place or friend,
   Smile of popularity.
The only honest politician,
   The only patriot is he
Who, in the face of opposition,
   Maintains thus his integrity,

TO PEACE.

Ne'er to right or left hand swerving,
 Living only for the right;
True hero he, and well deserving
 A place in Honour's palace bright.

TO PEACE.

CALM-VISAG'D Peace, O spirit bless'd!
 Within this agitated breast
 Come take up thy abode;
Diffuse thy beauteous mellow light,
And 'mid the darkness of the night
 Lead me o'er life's rough road.

Too long my soul hath been the nest
Of care, anxiety, unrest,
 With all their darksome brood;
O spirit, beautiful and kind,
People the cloister of my mind
 With thy sweet brotherhood!

For thee, thou pearl of greatest price,
My wounded heart would sacrifice
 All that mankind holds dear;
Rank, honour, riches, deathless fame,
If on my path thy sacred flame
 Might shine, a beacon clear.

Though lowly, insignificant,
With thee celestial visitant,
 Sojourning in my cot;
Though destitute of worldly good,
Enrich'd with thy sweet quietude,
 Most blessèd were my lot.

As He Who bade the waves be still,
And still'd their tumult at His will,
 Do thou, benignant Peace,
Breathe gently o'er my troubl'd breast,
Lull all my anxious fears to rest,
 Bid all my sorrows cease.

LITTLE SWEETHEART.

LITTLE sweetheart, why so cruel?
   Why look so disdainfully?
Brighter than the brightest jewel
   Are the eyes that rest on me,
Gazing with such icy scorn
On this sunny summer morn.

Little sweetheart, can'st not love me?
   See'st thou not my bitter woe;
Ah, how shall my poor words move thee,
   Warm that bosom white as snow;
At thy feet my heart I lay,
Dearest lov'd one, say not Nay.

Is it vain? Must I then leave thee?
   Hast thou then no love to give?
Well, I will not longer grieve thee,
   Though I know not how to live;
Little sweetheart, I depart,
With a sad, a broken heart.

O SING THOSE SONGS AGAIN.

O SING to me, my mother dear,
   In accents soft and low,
The songs that I so lov'd to hear
   In days of long ago;
As on my ear they gently fall
   They soothe me in my pain;
How sweet the memories they recall,
   O sing those songs again!

Yes, sing to me, my mother dear,
   Each old familiar strain,
Until in Fancy's vision clear
   I seem to see again
The dear lov'd ones of long ago
   On Memory's golden plain,
And I forget my present woe,
   O sing those songs again!

DAFFODILS.

PURE paly golden daffodils,
  The sight of you with pleasure fills
One's heart; while yet hiemal chills
Tenaciously are lingering,
Ye come, bright harbingers of spring,
Bringing with you a genial glow
Of warmth and rush of happiness,
The heart of man to cheer and bless.
'Tis sweet to see your yellow bells
Waving in the woodland dells;
Nature's sweet children pure and meek,
To fancy's ear ye seem to speak
With simple unaffected art,
And would that we within our heart
Did treasure up your pleasant lore;
Ye come to bring the priceless ore
Of purest and unmingl'd joy,
To find our powers sweet employ.
And as at you the pensive eye
Gazes, the mind is borne away,
And yielding unto Fancy's sway,
Flits on her magic pinions fleet
Through an enchanted region sweet,
Till, lost in rapture exquisite,
We rise above the wearying strain
Of earthly cares and worldly pain.
And thus, sweet children of the wood,
Ye are the ministers of good,
Speaking to us the power of Him,
Creation's God, the Lord Supreme;
Your tender forms with joy we greet,
And render you a tribute meet,
Of by-gone days ye sweetly tell;
Waft us to scenes remember'd well;
Our childhood's hour we live again,
Again we scour the grassy plain
And listen to the birds' sweet strain.
Heaven's beauteous mute messengers,
Bringing to us poor passengers

On this life's tempestuous sea
Bright gleams of Nature's radiancy;
Welcome, ye dryads of the dells,
Pale golden-crested daffodils.

IN THE GLOAMING.

SITTING musing in the gloaming
   By the ingle's ruddy glow,
Busy Fancy fondly roaming
   To the days of long ago;
What a troupe of mem'ries pleasant
   Visit us in lovely train,
Linking both the past and present
   In a beauteous golden chain!

Visions of our happy childhood,
   When in Life's bright morning beam
Roam'd we through the tangl'd wild wood
   Sported by the winding stream,
Gaily through the fragrant meadow
   Chas'd the flitting butterfly,
When no soul bedark'ning shadow
   Dimm'd the brightness of our sky.

Visions of a tender mother,
   Of a father kind and sage;
How we seem to see him turning
   O'er the Bible's sacred page!
A sister fair, a darling brother,
   All the friends so firm and true,
Gazing tenderly upon us
   Our fond fancy seems to view.

Glimpses of the dear departed,
   Visions sweet of bygone days,
Come to us when we're downhearted,
   Fainting on Life's rugged ways;
Be like guardian angels near us
   In the gloom of Sorrow's night,
Sent to strengthen and to cheer us,
   Guiding us to joy and light.

THE GIRL I LOV'D LONG YEARS AGO.

'TIS but a lock of flaxen hair,
   But O, how dear it is to me,
It oft recalls a vision fair
   Enshrined within my memory.
Earth holds for me no dearer thing ;
   Its power's secret would you know ?
It brings me back on Fancy's wing
   The girl I lov'd long years ago.

I see the little wicket gate—
   The dear familiar place of tryst—
Where my impatient heart did wait,
   And her fair face I fondly kiss'd ;
While all the myriad stars above
   Smil'd on two tender hearts below—
On me and on my beauteous love,
   The girl I lov'd long years ago.

I see her form of queenly grace
   Move lightly in the dreamy dance ;
Again I see her lovely face
   Blush brightly at my ardent glance.
No matter where I chance to be,
   She goes with me where'er I go ;
In vision sweet I ever see
   The girl I lov'd long years ago.

RULES OF LIFE.

ACT according to your light,
   Ever champion the right ;
Strive to keep a conscience clear,
Ever upright, true, sincere ;
Treasure all Life's fleeting hours ;
Labour to improve your powers,
Self-reliant, independent,
Aye to Duty's call attendant ;
Moderately drink of pleasure,
Usefully employ your leisure,
Violate no natural laws ;

Be not looking out for flaws
In another's mode of life ;
Shun all bickerings and strife ;
Honour give where it is due ;
Take not a one-sided view,
Truth's irradiating rays
Catch by looking various ways ;
On this world set no great store,
Of its riches seek no more
Than will satisfy your needs ;
Fill each day with noble deeds,
Thus ; whatever your position,
Be ye plebeian or patrician,
Acting in the living present,
Making life a picture pleasant
Deck'd in sweetly blending colours,.
God's obedient, willing scholars,
Carrying out His every teaching ;
All your aspirations reaching
Forward to a realm sublime,
Upward to a sinless clime
Far beyond the tomb and time.

CHRISTMAS IS HERE.

BORNE on Time's fleeting wing,
              Christmas is here !
Of Season's Chief and King,
              Christmas is here !
His jolly, ruddy face,
Beaming in every place,
Doth sorrow, care, displace,
              Christmas is here!

List to the chiming bells
              Christmas is here !
Their merry music tells
              Christmas is here !
To Childhood's bosom light,
To Youth, with visions bright,
To Age, with tresses white,
              Alike, how dear !

CHRISTMAS IS HERE.

Ring out your tidings glad,
          Christmas is here!
Tell to the poor, the sad,
          Christmas is here.
He comes for season brief,
Bringing a sweet relief,
Tell them to cease their grief—
          Christmas is here!

Bedeck the stately hall—
          Christmas is here!
The labourer's cottage small—
          Christmas is here!
Bring the green holly bough,
Where the red berries glow,
And the pale mistletoe—
          Christmas is here!

Time of re-unions sweet—
          Christmas is here!
Dear ones long parted meet—
          Christmas is here!
Some from the rolling brine,
From terra's central line
Homeward their steps incline
          From far and near.

Bid discord, malice cease—
          Christmas is here!
Let all be joy and peace—
          Christmas is here!
Ye rich in this world's good,
Out of your plenitude
Succour Earth's needy brood—
          Christmas is here.

List to the Christmas bells,
          Tuneful and clear!
Their cheering measure swells—
          Christmas is here!
Join we with heart and tongue
In the triumphant song,
The gladsome strain prolong—
          Christmas is here!

THE SEA.

I LOVE the sea, the grand wild sea,
   When the wind is whistling gay and free ;
I love it when fair morning breaks
O'er its blue face in orient streaks,
And Sol pours down his golden sheen ;
Superb and gorgeous is the scene.

I love to wander by the sea
When the wavelets murmur plaintively,
And the sportive sea-birds frequent rest
Upon its gently heaving breast,
That shines like a field of silver bright ;
Yes, the ocean then is a glorious sight.

And even when the tempest raves,
And boil and leap the giant waves,
Lifting their whiten'd crests on high
Until they seem to touch the sky;
Yes, the aspect of the stormy sea
Presents peculiar charms to me.

THE BUCCANEER.

A MERRY-HEARTED Buccaneer,
   Through mist and foam I gaily roam,
     Nor danger fear ;
Though winds may blow or high or low,
I laugh ha ! ha ! I laugh ho ! ho !
To friendly gales I spread my sails,
   And flit o'er ocean's blue expanse ;
I laugh ha ! ha ! I laugh ho ! ho !
   While song and dance my mirth enhance.
     Through Neptune's realms a ranger,
       Singing gaily.
     Though face to face with danger
       I am daily ;
     And when the storm is over,
       Tra-la-la,
     At ease reclines the rover,
       Tra-la-la ;

THE BUCCANEER.

Then with the magic music of my ha! ha! ha!
  Grim-visag'd Care I quickly drive away;
And I beg to intimate I'm prepared for any fate,
  For my heart is always gay.

When a wealthy prize comes in our way,
My gallant band with ready hand
  Attack their prey;
As the luckless foe goes down below,
I laugh ha! ha! I laugh ho! ho!
    With wealth untold of gleaming gold
    I tightly pack my vessel's hold;
    I laugh ha! ha! I laugh ho! ho!
    I and my vassals strong and bold;
    When attack'd by cruisers irate,
      True and ready, cool and steady
    They ever find this pirate,
      Ever ready;
    With courage, self-reliance
      Them I meet and defeat,
    And laugh in cool defiance
      As I see them retreat;
And when the fray is o'er, with my light guitar,
  To pleasure then I yield the happy day:
And my loud ha! ha! ringing near and far,
  Tells the Corsair's heart is gay.

All Love's entanglements I shun,
And venom'd fangs of jealous pangs;
    Each lovely one
  I love them all where'er I go,
  I laugh ha! ha! I laugh ho! ho!
  The blinded god projects his dart
  All vainly at the Corsair's heart.
    I laugh ha! ha! I laugh ho! ho'
  And mock at Beauty's wile and art.
  Their sighs I never heed 'em,
    Nor their anguish as they languish,
  But laugh in joyous freedom,
    As they seek me to vanquish;
  Like the wind, inconstant ever,
    I would roam, I would roam,

A mind like mine can never
   Rest at home.
I banish saucy Cupid with my ha! ha! ha!
   And acknowledge not the pretty tyrant's sway,
Marital felicity will never do me,
   For my heart is always gay.

I gaily sing from morn till night;
While others go through shades of woe
   My heart is light;
No ebb doth know my mirth's full flow;
I laugh ha! ha! Likewise ho! ho!
   A king I rule, my throne my deck,
   Of party warfare nought I reck;
I laugh ha! ha! I laugh ho! ho!
As like a bird my barque doth go:
   To the service of Queen Pleasure
      Do I daily
   Yield willingly my leisure,
      Singing gaily,
   As through her fairy palace
      I gallivant
   And taste her sparkling chalice
      Jubilant;
I never suffer trouble to disturb my peace,
   And to all my fellow mortals I would say;
Whether life be short or long, or things go right or wrong,
   Let the heart be always gay.

THE WIND.

I SING of the mysterious wind,
   Through Nature roaming unconfin'd,
Roving through the fragrant bowers,
Fondly dallying with the flowers,
A fitful friend, a faithless lover,
A swaggering, royst'ring, reckless rover,
Laughing, shrieking, whistling, whirling,
Sighing, sporting, raving, twirling
Round and round in courseless caper
Unoffending scraps of paper,

THE WIND.

Bullying the yellow leaves,
Moaning round the cottage eaves,
Sweeping o'er the sodden'd ground,
With a swirling rushing sound;
Murmuring plaintive minstrelsies
In and out the leafy trees,
Swaying the yellow-crested corn,
'Neath its onward rush o'erborne,
In the lonely woodland sighing,
Like the sound of mortal dying,
Riding on the restless sea,
Lashing its billows furiously,
Till they writhe and leap in pain,
Plunging full fathoms deep again,
Mocking the lightning's lurid flashing,
The dreaded thunder's horrid crashing,
Drowning the seaman's dying shriek,
Exulting o'er the yielding creak
As the feeble timbers break.
And now again thou'rt softly playing,
Athrough the lattice window straying,
The fever'd brow in coolness steeping
Of the tender infant sleeping.
O wondrous power strange and strong,
I love thy weird mysterious song;
Sometimes thou hast a soothing strain,
That falls like balm upon my pain,
Administ'ring a sweet relief;
Anon in melting tones of grief
Thou singest with unstudied art,
Till chords responsive in the heart
Vibrate; thou hast as many moods
As Earth's innumerable broods.
Mankind's e'er varying emotions
Are typified in thy commotions;
Thou'rt full of change, inconstancy,
So is our frail humanity,
And thou and we from day to day
Th' incomparable might display
Of Him Who rules with matchless skill
The whole creation at His will.

THE LITTLE MESSENGER.

A PRETTY little flower,
  Blooming all alone,
Fed by sun and shower,
  By soft breezes blown.

Distant from the highway,
  Hid from public view,
In a lonely by-way
  This little flower grew.

Growing discontented
  With its lowly state,
The flow'ret fair lamented
  Oft disconsolate.

Fretfully it murmured:
  "Mine's a luckless lot,
Secluded and unnotic'd
  In this lonely spot.

"What use is my beauty?
  Seldom passes by
Anyone to view me
  With admiring eye.

"Wasted is my perfume
  On the lone air shed,
I'm so very useless,
  Would that I were dead."

There came a little maiden
  One sunny summer day,
Her rosy arms were laden
  With leaves and flowers gay.

"O what a pretty flower"
  Delightedly cried she;
"I'm so glad I've found you;
  You must come with me."

The maiden in her posy
  Plac'd the little flower,
And laugh'd aloud in pleasure
  In the sunny hour.

Then soon her busy footsteps
    Carried her away
Into a darken'd chamber
    Where a sick man lay.

A strange young man, an exile
    From his native land;
She plac'd the rural beauty
    In his poor thin hand.

He gaz'd upon the flower
    With sorrow in his eye,
And from his heaving bosom
    Came a troubl'd sigh.

Thick o'er the fragile petals
    The tender teardrops fell
As Memory recall'd him
    Old times remember'd well.

His mother's fav'rite flower
    It was; and in a tone
Of wondrous moving power
    It spoke of her now gone.

It told of all her goodness
    To him, unceasing care;
Her days of loving labour,
    And nights of earnest prayer.

And then he saw her lying
    Upon her dying bed;
He heard as he stood crying
    The last fond words she said.

Again with poignant anguish
    He saw his life of sin;
With deep remorse reflected
    How wicked he had been.

And from his trembling bosom
    Uprose the humble plea—
" Against Thee have I sinned—
    Have mercy, Lord, on me."

And He Who never closes
  To contrite ones His ear
In gracious mercy sent him
  An answer to his prayer.

Then the poor weary wand'rer
  Sank peacefully to rest,
His mother's fav'rite flower
  Clasp'd tightly to his breast.

So the flower that lamented
  Within its lone abode
Became a guardian angel
  That led a soul to God.

EARTH AND HEAVEN.

EARTH hath many a pleasure fair,
  Many a sorrow, many a snare,
Hath many a trial hard to bear;
  Heaven hath rest from toil and care

Earth hath many a prospect bright,
Earth hath many a vain delight,
Many a labour, many a fight;
  Heaven hath realms of dimless light.

Earth hath many a pang of woe,
Earth hath many a cruel blow,
Earth hath many a deadly foe;
  No ills nor harms Heaven's people know.

Earth hath many a dazzling light,
Earth hath many a withering blight,
Many a painful sleepless night;
  Heaven hath ineffable delight.

Earth hath many a pleasure vain,
Many a dreary desert plain,
For nought oft times in toil we strain:
  Heaven hath incomparable gain.

Earth hath mingling sighs and tears,
Earth hath anxieties and fears,
Sad funeral bells, funereal biers;
  But Heaven hath painless deathless spheres.

HOPE.

OF all the gracious gifts that God
    Hath on the sons of men bestow'd
To aid them in Life's pilgrim way
None sweeter is than Hope's fair ray.

O sanguine sunny-hearted Hope,
Oft art thou as a timely rope
Flung to the soul that helplessly
Is borne on the tempestuous sea !

Thou comest deck'd in roseate light
Dispersing Sorrow's densest night,
When trouble with its circling gloom
Enfolds the heart as in a tomb.

The lab'ring man amid the moil
Of daily care and arduous toil
Experiences thy cheering power,
Anticipating the glad hour

When he shall to his home repair
And find sweet relaxation there.
Join in his children's artless glee
And taste home's deep felicity.

The soldier, too, amid the roar
Of battle's din, when cannon pour
Their deadly volleys far and wide,
Hopes for the time when War's red tide

Shall be roll'd back by gentle Peace
And battle's dreadful tumults cease :
When he may, scatheless from the strife,
Enfold again his own dear wife

Unto his manly faithful heart,
And from her breast extract the dart
Anxiety had planted there,
And see again his children dear.

The hope of safely reaching home
Cheers the bold fishers as they roam,
And mid the perils of the wave
Fills them with strength and makes them brave.

The invalid on bed of pain
Is cheer'd and bless'd oft and again
By visions sweet of rosy health,
That precious gift—Heaven's choicest wealth.

How doth the radiant spirit, too,
Paint to the toiling author's view
The golden region of success
His weary fainting soul to bless!

The merchant, too, whose eye doth range
With anxious gaze o'er the exchange,
Hopes ardently to realise
Large profits from his enterprise.

It nerves the timid lover's heart
And strength and courage doth impart,
As he essays in labour hard
To win his lov'd one's kind regard.

The student who in labours deep
Toileth while others calmly sleep,
Hopes for a guerdon for his pains—
A place in Learning's fair domains.

The husbandman with liberal hand
Soweth the seed within his land,
And hopes for sun and genial rain
To feed and fructify the grain.

How oft but for the cheering power
Would sink the spirit in the hour
Of dire distress when carking Care
Leads to the verge of dark Despair.

Thank Heav'n that sunny Hope is here,
Gilding the clouds that oft appear,
Sustaining the frail soul of man
As he pursues his measur'd span!

A LIFE THOUGHT.

BROTHER, do the best you can ;
   Envy not thy fellow man
If he wiser be than you ;
All may not be learn'd or clever ;
Have not the gifts nor the endeavour,
   Yet all may be kind and true ;
   All may Virtue's path pursue.

Brother, though in Learning's school
Thou may be esteem'd a fool,
   You may play a master part
In the grand academy
Of our vast humanity,
   With true refinement of the heart,
   Which scholar's lore cannot impart.

The noble with his garter'd knee,
His coronet and pedigree,
   In all the pride and pomp of state,
If heart and conduct be not right,
Is worthless in God's holy sight ;
   The virtuous alone are great,
   Whether of high or low estate.

To love is better than to sway ;
To win a soul from error's way
   Is better than to mount a throne ;
To mitigate earth's woes and pains
And bind in Love's soft silken chains
   Humanity from zone to zone
   Is work that Heaven will proudly own.

A GREETING.

YE busy scribes, afflicted with
   Cacoethes scribendi,
Ye roving gay Bohemian race,
   A friendly greeting send I ;
Bon camarades all, whate'er your theme,
   Verse, prose, or fact, or fiction,
Do not permit that vile word trite
   A place within your diction.

A GREETING.

With the thievish plagiaristic crew
    Make ye no compromise ;
But pure originality
    With deep affection prize ;
In borrow'd literary plumes
    Be not content to shine ;
But wear with pride your lowlier garb,
    Your own robes, if less fine.

Stick to your own particular style,
    Shun slavish imitation ;
Let not the thoughts of critics cause
    The slightest trepidation ;
With Nature as your one great book,
    Her pages bright your teachers,
Your only academic lore
    Her ever-varying features.

To win attention to your page,
    Exhaust your store of tactic ;
Adopt concise simplicity,
    But rarely be didactic ;
The thoughts that you would fain express
    Hide not with high-flown language
That makes the task of following you
    A source of cruel anguish.

The peacock, georgeous to the view,
    In plumage richly rare,
Emitteth a discordant note
    That jars upon the air ;
So oft, too, pompous prose or verse,
    Deck'd with pedantic art,
Breathes not the soul of music sweet—
    Its soul, its chiefest part.

Thus go your ways, my comrades all,
    Ye merry men of letters,
Scorning alike the smile or frown
    Of those your so-call'd betters ;
Dispensing in your varying spheres
    Truth's precious golden light,
And, never-wavering fealty swear
    To honour, justice, right.

"AVE MARIA."

'TIS Evening's hour sweetly fair;
   Upon the stilly balmy air
Softly ascends soft the holy prayer—
     Ave Maria.

Within the convent's peaceful ground
A solemn stillness reigns profound,
But broken by the sacred sound,
     Ave Maria.

Now meadow, copse, and fairy dell
Seem resting 'neath a holy spell;
Tinkles the distant shepherd's bell—
     Ave Maria.

The sinking sun's soft mellow smile
Rests on the wide cathedral aisle;
Rich music floods the noble pile—
     Ave Maria.

Pale Phœbe looks down from her height.
Her soft beam of approval bright
Blends with the altar's chasten'd light—
     Ave Maria.

To bow before th' Eternal Power
The noble from his princely tower,
The lowly come in this still hour—
     Ave Maria.

The roving Corsair, fierce and rude,
In humble penitential mood,
Bows down beneath the holy rood—
     Ave Maria.

It is the hour of Duty's call
From state intrigue or tavern brawl,
Gentle or simple, freeman, thrall—
     Ave Maria.

O mortals, snatch a respite brief
From earthly toils, from earthly grief;
Enjoy this hour of sweet relief,
     Ave Maria!

THE WORLD'S NEEDS.

HOW chang'd this world of ours would be
   If stead of strife and enmity
  And acrimonious railing,
Deep tender-hearted sympathy,
All comprehensive Charity,
  Were in our midst prevailing.

How swiftly Grief's discordant tones
Would vanish from our circling zones
  Disgusted and affrighted ;
Could mankind but be brought to see
Themselves as one vast family
  By Love's sweet bond united !

O would, O would our eyes but see
More artless frank simplicity
  In dealings with each other ;
Alas ! how grieving to perceive
Man striving, scheming to deceive
  His fellow and his brother.

How gladly also would we see
'Twixt practice and mere theory
  A more distinct connection ;
We see around us every day
Men contradict the good they say
  By some unworthy action.

Some parsons talk of brotherhood
In sermons eloquent and good
  From pulpits on the Sunday,
Then miserably fail to reach
The lofty standard that they teach
  By conduct on the Monday.

In our great Legislature too,
How much is there expos'd to view
  To set the spirit grieving ;
Men thinking more of " Party " claims
Than of the great and noble aims
  They ought to be achieving.

THE WORLD'S NEEDS.

What shameless deeds of cruel wrong,
The despotism of the strong,
   The sorrow and the sighing,
In terrible discordance rise,
Piercing the stillness of the skies;
   To Heav'n for vengeance crying!

O would we make allowance due
Whene'er our brethren's faults we view,
   And mingle with our judgment
Mercy's sweet "quality unstrain'd,"
How know we what might be attain'd,
   Our words may find a lodgement

In some forlorn less favour'd soul
O'er whom Temptation's billows roll
   With fell resistless power,
Our kindly word, our tender deed,
May bring forth, like the little seed,
   Some day a fruitful dower.

If Heav'n hath on us more bestow'd
Of light to guide us o'er Life's road
   Than on our weaker brother,
Let us be thankful for that light,
And use the precious beam aright
   And ne'er its radiance smother.

Then every thing ignobly mean,
All rancour, prejudice, and spleen,
   Foul slander and back-biting
Would o'er our peaceful happy shore
Diffuse their influence no more
   So withering and blighting.

Alas! alas! sad thought, that e'er
A world so wonderfully fair
   Man in his little hour,
By passion, pride, and selfishness,
By malice, anger, bitterness,
   To mar should have the power.

ENGLAND'S DUKE IS SATISFIED.

(On reading that the Duke of Cambridge had inspected the Forces and expressed himself as "quite satisfied.")

YE hardy sons of valiant Mars,
   With honour crown'd and battle's scars,
The glory of your native land,
The bulwarks of our power who stand;
List to my words, and swell with pride,
For Royal George is satisfied.

What matter it how critics carp
And on that old theme ever harp—
The shocking state of our defences
And annual growth of their expenses-
These pessimistic souls we'll chide,
Since England's Duke is satisfied.

Though bay'nets break and sabres bend,
And many a gallant fellow send
Before his time beneath the sod,
What if our big guns oft explode
And lay more of our own men low
Than of the swarthy-visag'd foe;
Ne'er heed how critics may deride,
Is not George Ranger satisfied?

Then let us rest with calm belief,
And breathe a sigh of sweet relief,
To feel assur'd that all is right;
That we can rest us of a night,
And not dread waking in the morn ;
These jaundic'd croakers we will scorn
And beam with calm complacent pride,
Since England's Duke is satisfied.

ONLY AN OLD OLD DITTY.

ONLY an old old ditty
   Sung in a crowded street
Of London's mighty city,
   In falt'ring tones but sweet,
By a little bright-eyed fair-hair'd child,
A waif in the social desert wild.

Only an old old ditty,
　　But, listening to the strain
Sung by the minstrel pretty,
　　What mem'ries live again,
Awaken'd by a simple song
Sung to a sympathetic throng !

Only an old old ditty,
　　No brilliant lyric flower,
In language grand or witty,
　　Yet full of subtle power
To hold and move the human heart
With untaught but resistless art.

Only an old old ditty,
　　Yet through those standing by
There throbs a thrill of pity,
　　While scarce an eye is dry—
Meet homage of a gather'd throng
To the power of a simple song.

THE HOURS OF LIFE.

WASTE not the precious hours of life
　　On transitory, worldly pleasures ;
Spend not your powers in the strife
　　For perishing material treasures ;
But seek for more enduring things—
　　That leave no memories to grieve you,
For solid gains that take not wings,
　　Like earthly riches, which oft leave you ;
Treasures of Faith, of Hope, and Love,
　　Heaven's glad joy for earthly sorrow :
Beauteous visions from above,
　　Glimpses of a bright to-morrow
In a better world than this,
　　Where there is no sin, no sadness,
A realm of never-ending bliss,
　　Never-ceasing songs of gladness.
Life's too earnest, far too short,
　　To pass in idle, aimless dreaming,
In follies, or in sinful sport,
　　Or sordid, avaricious scheming.
Strive, O strive to leave the world

Better, purer than you found it;
Jehovah's banner floats unfurl'd,
　Brethren, up and rally round it!
Inaugurate a new Crusade
　'Gainst all the varied forms of evil,
God's foes, against the truth array'd,
　The sinful world, the flesh, the devil.
Thus pass ye through Life's pilgrim way
　Of the Master's will observant;
At the last your Lord shall say:—
　" Well done! good and faithful servant."

SONNETS.—THE CUCKOO.   MAY.

WELCOME, thou wanderer from land remote,
　E'er welcome, gentle harbinger of Spring!
Cheering to us thy sweet though plaintive note.
　To us rich pleasure doth thy advent bring;
Bright pictures ting'd with promise fair of May,
　Her snowy hedgerows, meadows freshly green,
With early flowerets making Nature gay,
　The matchless sun with his irradiant sheen.
Dear bird, thou com'st to sound the passing knell
　Of tyrant Winter; starting at thy voice,
Chagrin'd he calls away from hill and dell
　His vassals rude; earth greatly doth rejoice
To see him go with sullen parting roar,
And Spring's sweet voice proclaims his reign is o'er.

And see! where cometh smiling rosy May,
　For season sweet to dominate the scene;
A spirit fair in beauteous array,
　On her pure brow a chaplet emerald green;
On her white bosom many a brilliant gem
　Sparkles; rich odours impregnate the air;
Bright Flora weaves a lovely diadem
　To decorate her handmaid passing fair;
Rich strains of music o'er the welkin float,
　As feather'd choirs in untaught minstrelsy
Enraptur'd hymn her praise with fullest throat;
　While zephyrs dance around in sportive glee;
O'er the grand prospect rings a thrilling voice
Crying, May has come; rejoice, O earth, rejoice!

PATRIOTISM.

WHO is the genuine patriot? Is it he
    Who pins his faith to conquest and to might?
And vainly thinks true *amor patriæ*
    But breathes in those who in the gory fight
And pomp of armed battalia take delight?
    Who glories in grim battle's lurid flames,
With ardour climbs the reeking gory height,
    To whom this life presents no nobler aims
Than winning decorations, men's applause,
    A niche perchance in Glory's gilded fane,
Too oft, alas! regardless if the cause
    Be such as Honour, Justice, Truth approve;
Indifferent to the misery and pain
    That mark the path wherein red Mars doth move?

Is not the genuine patriot rather he
    Who in fair Honour's teachings doth delight?
And in his inmost soul desires to see
    His country sway'd by dictates pure, upright?
Who fondly strives to spread the arts of peace,
    And nightly breathes to Heav'n the fervent prayer
That Righteousness may mightily increase,
    Rich Plenty yield to toil a guerdon fair;
That man may learn to love his fellow-man,
    The human race in Learning e'er advance,
All in accord with Nature's noble plan,
    Fair Knowledge bending down her kindly glance,
Religion rear in every heart a throne,
And love and joy prevail from zone to zone.

TO A DISAPPOINTED GENIUS.

DO you wonder, my poor brother,
    Why your merits are pass'd by;
Why you toil long years in patience,
    But to heave the bitter sigh,
Wearied out and disappointed,
    Your exertions all in vain;
All your soul-absorbing labour
    So much unrewarded pain?

TO A DISAPPOINTED GENIUS.

Do you wistfully look round you
   For some sympathetic soul
That can understand your feelings,
   Help you onward to your goal?
Have you found those who though warmest
   In your praise day after day
Would not lift their little finger
   To assist you on your way?

Thick as leaves in Vallambrosa
   People scatter words of praise;
It is easy, words cost nothing,
   But appeal to them to raise
Something rather more substantial,
   Soon you'll see the proof most clear;
Your remarks are only falling
   On a deaf unwilling ear.

Yes, they'd rather spend their money
   On a statue to the dead,
Than they'd try to help the living;
   Yes, what copious tears they shed
O'er the poor souls they neglected
   Who have trod this mundane round;
They can better see their merits
   When they're underneath the ground.

Think of that most wondrous genius—
   The incomparable Burns,
Whose bright name shall live as long as
   Terra on her axis turns.
Now, to sing his worth and praises
   Language Mercury outvies,
All they found for him when living
   Was a place in the Excise.

So you see, my weary brother,
   What a genius must expect—
Vapid, empty, fulsome praises;
   Solid, practical neglect.
Then if you would have your merits
   Brought before the public eye,
If you'd have them do you justice,
   All you have to do is—die.

www.ingramcontent.com/pod-product-compliance
Lightning Source LLC
Chambersburg PA
CBHW021727220426
43662CB00008B/731